INTRODUCTION *to* BUSINESS

Fifth Edition

Instructor's Manual

JEFF MADURA
FLORIDA ATLANTIC UNIVERSITY

Paradigm
PUBLISHING

St. Paul   Los Angeles   Indianapolis

Care has been taken to verify the accuracy of information presented in this book. However, the authors, editors, and publisher cannot accept responsibility for Web, e-mail, newsgroup, or chat room subject matter or content, or for consequences from application of the information in this book, and make no warranty, expressed or implied, with respect to its content.

ISBN 978-0-76383-621-4

© 2010 by Paradigm Publishing, Inc.
875 Montreal Way
St. Paul, MN 55102
E-mail: educate@emcp.com
Web site: www.emcp.com

Printed in the United States of America

18 17 16 15 14 13 12 11 10 09   1 2 3 4 5 6 7 8 9 10

TABLE OF CONTENTS

Chapter 1: Functions of a Business

Introduction

The **Learning Objectives** for this chapter are to:

1. Explain the motives of a business.

2. Identify the resources a business use to produce a product or service.

3. Identify the key stakeholders who are involved in a business.

4. Describe the business environment to which a firm is exposed.

5. Describe the key types of business decisions.

1. Motives of a Business
If an owner of a business can provide a product or service that is desired by customers, it may be able to:
- Increase Satisfaction Level of Consumers
- Create Jobs for Employees
- Generate Profits

1.1 How a Business Generates Profits

1.2 Conditions That Affect Business Profits
* The profit motive is influenced by the government.

1.3 Motive of Nonprofit Businesses
A nonprofit organization serves a specific cause and is not intended to make profits, but is run like a business.

2. Resources Used by Businesses

2.1 Natural Resources — any resources that can be used in their natural form

2.2 Human Resources — people

2.3 Capital — machinery, equipment, tools, and physical facilities
- Technology helps businesses improve their capital.

- E-commerce uses electronic communications to produce or sell products or services.

2.4 Entrepreneurship — creation of business ideas and willingness to accept risk

3. Key Stakeholders in a Business

3.1 Owners (entrepreneurs) start a business as the result of ideas about a product or service. The entrepreneur organizes, manages, and assumes the risks associated with operating a business. As a business grows, additional owners may be needed, and the business may ultimately go public by issuing stock to investors (stockholders).

3.2 Creditors are financial institutions or individuals who loan funds to a business. The firm must pay interest on the amount borrowed. Creditors will loan funds to a firm that will likely be able to repay the loan.

3.3 Employees are individuals who work for a firm. Managers are employees who are responsible for making key business decisions and overseeing the work of other employees. The goal of the managers of a firm is maximize the value of the firm.

3.4 Suppliers provide the materials required to produce products.

3.5 Customers buy the products produced by firm.

3.6 Summary and Interaction Among Stakeholders: Firms receive funds from owners, creditors, and customers. They use some of the funds received to pay back loans, to pay employees, and to pay suppliers. They may also pay owners a portion of the profit as dividends.

4. The Business Environment

4.1 The **social environment** reflects demographics, or characteristics of the population, which affect the demand for a firm's products.

4.2 The **industry environment** reflects the competition. Intense competition can adversely affect a business.

4.3 The **economic environment** affects consumer demand for products and therefore affects business performance.

4.4 The **global environment** affects consumer demand for products. Global competition can affect the firm's sales.

5. Key Types of Business Decisions

The key types of business decisions may be classified as management, marketing, and finance.

- **Management** is the means by which employees and other resources are used by a firm.
- **Marketing** is the means by which products or services are developed, priced, distributed, and promoted to customers.
- **Finance** is the means by which a firm obtains and uses funds for its business operations.

5.1 How Business Decisions Affect Performance

5.2 How Businesses Rely on Information

Accounting and information systems are used to facilitate business decisions. Accounting summarizes and analyzes financial information. Information systems can be used to update and analyze information about a firm's operations.

5.3 Applying the Key Types of Decisions to a Single Business

Solutions to End-of-Chapter Exercises

Concept Review Questions

(1) Motive. What is a motive for creating a business? What is the risk of creating a business?

The goal of a business is to provide a product or service that is desired by customers, enabling it to make a profit. Entrepreneurs who create a business may not only satisfy customers, but also may satisfy themselves by working in a business that they created.

The risk of creating a business is that you may lose all the money that you invest in a business.

(2) Profits and Business Value. How does a business generate a profit? How can profits be measured? Why do higher profits result in a higher business value?

A business generates revenue from selling its product. It incurs expenses from producing and marketing its product. The difference between its revenue and expenses over a period of time is the profits. When profits rise, this enhances the wealth of the owners. A business that generates more profits over time provides more wealth to the owners and therefore is more valuable. If a business is sold, its selling price will be influenced by the potential profits that it could generate for the future owners.

(3) Competition. Explain how the profit motive for businesses ensures that many businesses are created to satisfy all preferences by customers. How can the profit motive ensure that there will be sufficient competition among businesses? Why is this beneficial to customers?

The profit motive encourages entrepreneurs to start businesses because by satisfying customer needs, they generate sales and can make profits. If only one business sells specific product and the price is very high, other businesses will enter the market and offer a lower price in order to attract demand. Thus, this competition is beneficial to customers because they will pay a lower price as a result.

(4) Stakeholders. Describe the roles of the five key stakeholders in a business.

- An entrepreneur creates a business as a result of an idea for a product or service. The entrepreneur organizes, manages, and assumes the risks associated with operating the business. As the business grows, additional owners may be needed, and the business may ultimately go public by issuing stock to investors (stockholders).

- Creditors are financial institutions or individuals who loan funds to a business. The firm must pay interest on the amount borrowed. Creditors will loan funds to a firm that will likely be able to repay the loan.

- Employees are individuals who work for a firm. Managers are employees who are responsible for making key business decisions and overseeing the work of other employees. The goal of the managers of a firm is maximize the value of the firm.

- Suppliers provide the materials required to produce products.

- Customers buy the products produced by firm.

(5) Reliance on Resources. Explain the resources that you would need if you started a small business.

You may rely on natural resources (such as land), which can be used in their natural form. You may need human resources to help with production and other tasks. You may need capital (machinery, equipment, tools, and physical facilities) to produce the products. You may also rely on entrepreneurship, in order to create business ideas and take risks.

(6) Financing. Describe the role of financing for a business as it expands.

As a business expands, its earnings may not be sufficient to support the amount of desired expansion. Thus, it will attempt to obtain funds from other investors or from creditors such as financial institutions or individuals who loan funds to a business. The firm must pay interest on the amount borrowed. Creditors will loan funds to a firm that will likely be able to repay the loan. As a business grows, additional owners may be needed, and the business may ultimately go public by issuing stock to investors.

(7) Creditors. Why do you think it is difficult for some small businesses to obtain funding from creditors?

Creditors provide funding only if they have confidence that their loans will be repaid. Many small businesses fail and are unable to repay any loans. Thus, creditors must assess the likelihood that a business will be able to repay its loans.

(8) Business Decisions. Describe the key types of decisions involved in running a business. Explain how you would apply these decisions if you owned a business that produces bicycles.

- Management decides what resources are needed to produce the product.

- Marketing focuses on the target market for the firm's products or services. The marketing function is also involved in making decisions regarding product characteristics, pricing, distribution, and promotion.

- Finance attempts to provide the necessary funds to enable the firm to achieve its mission. These funds may come from the issuance of stock or from borrowing money.

These decisions are supported by:

- Accounting provides the information necessary to assess the performance of previous management, marketing, and finance decisions.

- Information systems provide the computerized communication system to continually update and analyze the firm's operations. It includes the information technology, people, and procedures that work together to provide appropriate information to the firm's employees.

You rely on management decisions to determine the process of producing bicycles. You rely on marketing strategies to sell bicycles. You need financing to cover the cost of production and marketing.

(9) Business Environment. Explain the various ways in which the performance of a business is affected by the environment.

- The social environment reflects demographics, or characteristics of the population, which affect the demand for a firm's products.

- The industry environment reflects the competition. Intense competition can adversely affect a business.

- The economic environment affects consumer demand for products and therefore affects business performance.

- The global environment affects consumer demand for products. Global competition can affect the firm's sales.

(10) Business Functions. Describe how management, marketing, and financing would be necessary if you started your own pizza delivery service.

Management is needed to hire and manage employees who would deliver pizzas. Marketing is necessary to promote and advertise your service. Financing is necessary to obtain the funds to start your business.

Class Communication Questions

(1) Being a Manager Versus Owner. You have a choice of being the primary manager (without any ownership) or the owner of a very small business. Would you have more to gain if you were the manager or the owner? Would you have more to lose if you were the manager or the owner?

The manager may benefit from having a good salary, but the owner will receive the profits after paying expenses. The owner normally has more to gain. However, the owner may need to reinvest the profits in the firm while the manager does not have to worry about investing in the business. As the owner, you could lose your entire investment in the business. As manager, you would not have funds invested in the business, but you could lose your job if the business performs poorly.

(2) Obtaining Funds from Creditor Versus Owner. You own a small business and need some financing. You could either borrow $20,000 or allow an investor to invest $20,000 in your business and become a part-owner. You expect that your business will be very profitable this year. Would you prefer to finance the business by borrowing or by allowing someone to become part-owner of your business?

By borrowing, you will have to make periodic interest payments to the creditor, whereas you would not need to provide such payments to a part-owner. But, if you borrow funds, you remain the sole owner, so that all profits will be yours. You would have to make the payment on the loan, but given that you expect the business to perform well, you should prefer to remain the sole owner.

(3) Importance of Management Versus Marketing. Assume you own a small clothing store at the mall, and consider the key management and marketing functions for this store. Do you think the store's management or marketing function would have a bigger influence on the performance of the business?

The store's management functions may involve the efficient use of employees in the store. The marketing function would involve promoting the store in order to generate more customer interest and sales. An argument could be made for either function.

Small Business Case — Key Decisions for Business Success

Emma Murray created a business called 4-Eyes DVD Rental because she recognized that customers desired a product that she could provide. To start this business, she borrowed some money from her sister and received an investment from her parents, who are co-owners of the business. In order to have a successful business, Emma needed to offer products desired by customers, and keep her expenses low so that she could price her DVD rentals low and still make a profit. She believed she could offer a wider selection of DVDs at a lower price than the only other DVD rental outlet in town. She also can keep her rent expenses low by renting store space in an area of midprice stores rather than in the exclusive shopping mall where the competitor DVD rental shop is located.

(1) How the Product Affects Success. Explain how the decision by Emma to offer DVD rentals rather than other types of products will influence the success of her new business.

> The demand for the product sold by a business varies with the product. The level of competition also varies with the product. In this case, the firm offers a DVD rental service that is desired by many customers and is offered by only one other firm in town.

(2) How the Pricing Affects Success. Explain how the decision by Emma to offer DVD rentals at a relatively low price will influence the success of the business.

> The price charged for a product influences the demand by customers and the revenue generated by a business. If the price charged for a product is too high, customers will purchase the product from another firm. However, the firm must charge a price that will be above the expense of offering the product.

(3) How Factors of Production Affect Success. What is the danger of this business hiring too many employees?

> When a business hires more employees than it needs, it incurs higher expenses than are necessary, which will reduce its profits.

(4) How Stakeholders Benefit from Business Success. How does the performance of this business affect the co-owners (Emma's parents) or the creditor (Emma's sister) who provided funding to start the business?

> High performance will ensure that the creditor's loan is repaid and that the co-owners earn a good return on their investment.

Web Insight — Business Functions at YouTube

The business YouTube was introduced at the beginning of this chapter. Review its website (www.youtube.com) as you answer these questions. What resources are needed to run YouTube? Describe the key stakeholders of YouTube. In October 2006, Google acquired YouTube for $1.65 billion. Why do you think YouTube is valued so high? That is, how can YouTube generate large profits that will make Google's investment worthwhile?

> YouTube relies on human resources (employees) to make sure the website is working properly and to improve the website in response to customer preferences. It relies on technology to make the website function.

> The key stakeholders of YouTube are its employees, its owners (shareholders), and its customers.

> YouTube attracts a very large number of viewers. Thus, it has the opportunity to allow firms to advertise to these viewers. The advertisers pay YouTube for advertising on YouTube's website.

Dell's Secret for Success

Go to Dell's website (www.dell.com) and click on the link "About Dell," near the bottom of the web page. You can also review a recent annual report of Dell for more information.

(1) Unique Business Idea. When Michael Dell started the business in 1984, he focused on building relationships directly with customers, as explained on Dell's website. Explain how this business idea differed from those of other computer manufacturers.

> Dell's business was designed to serve customers directly, without the need for retail stores to sell its computers. This could avoid a markup from retailers and please customers. The business could also allow for computers to be customized to satisfy customer preferences.

(2) Goals. How does Dell describe its goals in its annual report as they relate to its customers? To its employees? To its shareholders? Are these goals related? Explain.

> Dell wants to ensure that its customers are satisfied, that it is an exceptional place for its employees to work, and that it provides superior returns to its shareholders. All of these goals are related. By satisfying its employees, it ensures that they serve the needs of the customers. By providing quality products at fair prices to its customers, it attracts a very strong demand for its products, which results in high sales. It runs its business efficiently to maintain costs at a low level.

(3) Appeal to Stakeholders. How do Dell's stockholders gain from the attention that Dell gives to its customers and its employees?

Dell recognizes that it needs to give attention to customers and employees in order to be successful. Dell will perform better if it can satisfy its customers and employees, and this will result in a higher return to its shareholders.

Video Exercise — Lessons in Starting a Business

Many free business videos are available on websites such as YouTube (www.youtube.com), and more are added every day. Search for a recent video clip about an existing business that offers lessons on "starting your own business" in YouTube or any other website that provides video clips.

(1) Main Lesson. What is the name of the business in the video clip? Does the video focus on the owners, creditors, employees, suppliers, or customers? What is the main lesson of the video clip that you watched?

> Answers will vary among students. The question is designed to ensure that students take the initiative to access and watch a related video, and recognize the main lesson provided by the video.

(2) Bad Business Decisions. Some related videos suggest that a many businesses fail because they made poor decisions about their product. Other videos say that many businesses fail because they made poor decisions about hiring employees. Yet, some other videos suggest that businesses fail because they did not ensure adequate financing. Which of these lessons do you think is most important?

> Any of these possible answers is reasonable, but in reality a business must avoid all of these situations. In general, a business needs to offer a product that has some features beyond what other products offer (or has a lower price), hire good employees, and obtain adequate financing. If it fails at any one of these tasks, the business may fail.

(3) Power Struggle. Business videos commonly suggest that an entrepreneur has trouble giving up power, which restricts the ability to grow. Yet, there are also cases in which the entrepreneur gave too much responsibility to employees. Describe the tradeoff.

> If entrepreneurs do the most basic tasks, they have less time to manage other parts of the business. They limit their time devoted to planning the growth of the business. If they would allow employees some responsibility, they could use their time to plan for growth, create new products, etc. However, if they give too much responsibility to employees and the employees are not capable, this may adversely affect the business performance.

Chapter 2: Business Ethics and Social Responsibility

Introduction

The **Learning Objectives** for this chapter are to:

1. Describe the responsibilities of firms to their customers.

2. Describe the responsibilities of firms to their employees.

3. Describe the responsibilities of firms to their stockholders.

4. Describe the responsibilities of firms to their creditors.

5. Describe the responsibilities of firms to the environment.

6. Describe the responsibilities of firms to their communities.

1. Responsibility to Customers

1.1 Responsible Production Practices — to ensure customer safety

1.2 Responsible Sales Practices — to prevent deceptive sales strategies or deceptive advertising

1.3 How Firms Ensure Their Responsibility
- Establish a code of responsibilities that sets guidelines for product quality.
- Monitor complaints from customers regarding the quality of the product. Correct any deficiencies that are detected from customer feedback.
- Obtain customer feedback on the products or services customers have recently purchased, even if the customers did not complain. Correct any deficiencies that are detected from customer feedback.

1.4 How the Government Ensures Responsibility
- Regulation of product safety is enforced by government agencies such as the Food and Drug Administration (FDA).
- Regulation of advertising to prevent deceptive advertising.
- Regulation of industry competition ensures intense competition among firms because it forces firms to charge lower prices and provide better quality products in order to compete effectively for customer business.

2. Responsibility to Employees

2.1 Employee Safety
Firms monitor their production process to ensure a safe working environment.

2.2 Proper Treatment by Other Employees
Firms attempt to ensure a diverse workplace and also attempt to prevent sexual harassment by other employees.

2.3 How Firms Ensure Their Responsibility Toward Employees
- Code of responsibility
- Grievance policy for employees
- Job satisfaction initiatives

2.4 Conflict with Employee Layoffs
Employee layoffs may be necessary to maximize firm value.

2.5 How the Government Ensures Responsibility to Employees
Laws protect against discrimination and sexual harassment.

3. Responsibility to Stockholders

3.1 How Firms Ensure Responsibility to Stockholders
- Align compensation with the firm's value so that managers make decisions that are in the best interests of the stockholders.
- Conflict of interests — Tying employee compensation to the firm's value can create a conflict of interest by encouraging managers to distort financial reporting just before they sell their stock holdings.

3.2 How the Government Ensures Responsibility
The Sarbanes-Oxley Act requires more thorough financial reporting and holds executives and board members accountable for reporting errors.

3.3 How Stockholders Ensure Responsibility
- **Shareholder activism** refers to the active role that stockholders take to influence a firm's management policies. **Institutional investors** (financial institutions that purchase stock) can have major influence because they hold much stock.
- Excessive executive compensation can be in conflict with maximizing the firm's value because it raises expenses.

4. Responsibility to Creditors
Firms must repay loans from creditors in a timely manner.

4.1 How Some Firms Violate Their Responsibility
Firms mislead creditors when they provide misleading financial information.

5. Responsibility to the Environment

5.1 Air Pollution
- Firms reduced air pollution by refining their production processes.
- Government guidelines reduced air pollution.

5.2 Land Pollution

5.3 Conflict with Environmental Responsibility
Firms incur expenses when they reduce pollution, which could reduce profits for the owners.

6. Responsibility to the Community
Firms sponsor local events and donate to local charities.

6.1 Serving the Community and Stockholders
Maximizing social responsibility may conflict with the goal of maximizing a firm's profits for its owners. Firms seek a compromise in which they invest money in the community in ways that may ultimately increase their reputation and therefore sales.

7. Summary of Business Responsibilities

7.1 Business Responsibilities in an International Environment

7.2 The Cost of Fulfilling Social Responsibilities

8. How the Chapter Concepts Affect Business Performance

Solutions to End-of-Chapter Exercises

Concept Review Questions

(1) Responsibility to Stakeholders. Explain how a firm's responsibility to its stakeholders can affect its performance and value.

If a firm demonstrates its responsibility to its stakeholders, it will gain their trust. Thus, it will have a good reputation with customers. This results in higher revenue (from more sales). Its responsibility to employees will enable it to motivate employees and should result in lower expenses. Thus, it will achieve higher performance, higher profits, and a higher business value.

(2) Responsibility to Customers and Employees. Explain how businesses have a responsibility to employees.

Businesses have a responsibility toward their employees to ensure their workplace safety, proper treatment by other employees, and equal opportunity.

(3) Motivating Employees. How can firms motivate managers to maximize the value of the firm by tying employee compensation to a firm's performance? Explain why this strategy is not always effective.

A firm can provide its managers with shares of the firm's stock as partial compensation, so that managers are directly rewarded for making decisions that increase the value of the stock. However, managers may be tempted to exaggerate the financial reporting when they want to sell their shares, because they could make investors believe that the firm is performing better than it really is. This would allow them to sell the stock at a relatively high price.

(4) Satisfying Employees Versus Owners. Consider a firm that is suffering losses and has more employees than it needs. Explain the dilemma for managers who try to satisfy the owners of the firm and also try to satisfy the employees.

The firm may need to lay off some employees in order to reduce its expenses and to survive. However, this will reduce the morale of employees. If the managers do not lay off employees, they are not maximizing the firm's value because the expenses are excessive given that there are too many employees.

(5) Responsibility to Owners. Explain how businesses have a responsibility to their owners.

Firms monitor manager's decisions to ensure that the managers make decisions that are in the best interests of the owners (i.e., maximizing the firm's value). Shareholder activism is one way that stockholders ensure responsibility.

(6) Responsibility to Creditors. Explain how businesses have a responsibility to their creditors.

Firms are also responsible for repaying loans to creditors and should provide accurate financial information to creditors.

(7) Responsibility to the Environment. Explain how businesses have a responsibility to the environment.

Firms sometimes damage the environment with their production processes. They have refined their processes to reduce pollution. Firms face a conflict in some cases because they realize that spending money to reduce pollution can reduce their profits.

(8) Government Laws. How does the government attempt to ensure that firms are socially responsible to customers?

The government imposes laws in order to ensure that:
a. products are safe for customers.
b. advertising by firms to customers is not deceptive.
c. there is competition among businesses, as competition will provide consumers with higher quality goods and services at lower prices.

(9) Responsibility to Community. Describe the firm's responsibility toward its community.

Firms can show their concern for the community by sponsoring local events or donating to local charities.

(10) Impact of Lawsuits. Explain why potential lawsuits against firms should motivate firms to be socially responsible.

Lawsuits by customers or employees against firms can be very expensive. To the extent that being socially responsible can prevent some of the lawsuits, it can save the firm money.

Class Communication Questions

(1) Ethics of a Pricing Policy. Many car dealerships set the price of a car at a higher level than they are willing to sell the car. Customers who do not understand the car dealership's pricing process will pay more than other customers. Is this pricing policy ethical?

Some students would suggest that this pricing process is not ethical because it means that some customers will pay higher prices if they do not understand car dealership strategies. Yet, there are many case of products in which less informed customers pay higher prices, so some students may suggest that it is the responsibility of the customer to have adequate information before purchasing a car.

(2) Ethics of a Hiring Decision. You are a manager of a business. Is it fair for you to hire your friends instead of other applicants? Discuss.

In reality, some students would likely hire their friends. They may explain that they need to help their friends, and they may not necessarily view their decision as unethical. While they are just trying to help a friend, and are not directly stealing from the business, their decision could adversely affect the performance and value of the business. If students are placed in the position of the business owner, they may change their opinion.

(3) Ethics of a Loan Application. You need funds to start your business. You will need to show a creditor your business plan when you apply for a loan. You will only receive the loan if you convince creditors that you will be able to repay the loan. Should you exaggerate your expectations of your business performance in order to ensure that you receive a loan?

Students may argue that they need to lie in order to obtain the funding that they deserve and that they would be willing to repay the loan. Yet, the creditor deserves to have accurate information about the applicant. If students are placed in the position of the creditor, they may change their answer.

Small Business Case — Responsibilities of a Business

Cool Jewel Company sells costume jewelry. Its sales people receive a commission based on the amount of products that they sell. The business attempts to meet social responsibilities in the following ways. It warns the sales people that they must tell customers that the jewelry is not real gold. It has established guidelines to ensure fair treatment toward employees. It provides safety training to employees who make the jewelry. It also has a policy stating that sexual harassment will not be tolerated. It relies on creditors for funding. It plans to do some community service in order to increase its visibility. It considered giving cash awards for accomplishments by people in the community. Alternatively, it considered providing jewelry that has its name inscribed on it to these people.

(1) Responsibility to Customers. How can honest sales practices result in higher sales over time?

As a result of honest sales practices, the customers may trust the sales people and may come back to buy more jewelry over time.

(2) Responsibility to Employees. Why might Cool Jewel's policies for employees reduce employee turnover and expenses?

Its policies ensure a better working environment, which reduces turnover and therefore reduces expenses associated with hiring and training new employees.

(3) Responsibility to Creditors. Cool Jewel has borrowed some funds from creditors in the past. Why would the owner fulfill the company's obligations to creditors before granting himself a bonus?

The owner must satisfy the creditors because the company is obligated to pay creditors what it owes them on a timely basis.

(4) Responsibility to the Community. If Cool Jewel wants to increase its visibility, should it give cash awards for accomplishments by people in the community, or should it provide free jewelry that has its name inscribed to these people?

If Cool Jewel provides free jewelry, the recipients will likely show the gifts to their friends. Therefore, the company is able to advertise its name and the type of jewelry that it produces by providing free jewelry to people for specific accomplishments in the community.

Web Insight — Social Responsibilities at Starbucks

At the opening of the chapter, Starbucks was introduced. Review its website (www.starbucks .com) and the link to the year in review (or the link to its most recent annual report). Summarize comments made about Starbucks' social responsibilities to its customers, employees, or environment.

Starbucks describes its efforts to please customers, its benefits package for employees, and its focus on improving education in the community.

Dell's Secret for Success

Go to Dell's website (www.dell.com) and click on the link "About Dell," near the bottom of the web page. Review the section called "Values." You can also review a recent annual report of Dell for more information.

(1) Goals. Describe Dell's goals with respect to the communities where it works.

Dell is committed to serving its communities.

(2) Donations. Briefly summarize Dell's efforts to improve the environment.

Dell and its employees have donated millions of dollars to various charities. They have allocated thousands of hours to volunteer for various community events.

(3) Code of Conduct. Summarize Dell's corporate responsibilities to its employees and customers.

It is attempting to ensure good products and service for customers and a pleasant and safe environment for employees.

Video Exercise — Lessons in Business Ethics

Many free business videos are available on websites such as YouTube (www.youtube.com), and more are added every day. Search for a recent video clip about an existing business that offers lessons on "business ethics" in YouTube or any other website that provides video clips.

(1) Main Lesson. What is the name of the business in the video clip? Is the video clip focused on the firm's responsibility to its customers, employees, stockholders, creditors, or the environment? What is the main lesson of the video clip that you watched?

Answers will vary among students. The question is designed to ensure that students take the initiative to access and watch a related video, and recognize the main lesson provided by the video.

(2) Improper Treatment. Why do you think some firms do not offer proper treatment to their customers or their employees or to the environment?

Firms incur expenses when they treat their customers properly with safe products or good service. They incur expenses when they provide employees with proper work conditions or when they prevent pollution. Some firms may attempt to avoid these expenses, but they will develop a bad reputation for their mistreatment (or even penalties by the government), so their strategy tends to backfire.

(3) Benefits of Business Ethics. A common lesson in related videos is that good business ethics pays off. Explain how firms can enhance their performance when they make the effort to treat their customers and employees well.

The businesses are able to retain customers when they treat customers well, and this may result in higher sales and revenue. They are able to retain good employees when they treat them well, and this may result in lower expenses because they have less employee turnover.

Chapter 3: Assessing Economic Conditions

Introduction

The **Learning Objectives** for this chapter are to:

1. Explain how economic growth affects business performance.

2. Explain how inflation affects business performance.

3. Explain how interest rates afect business performance

4. Explain how market prices are determined.

5. Explain how the government influences economic conditions.

1. Impact of Economic Growth on Business Performance

1.1 Strong Economic Growth
When growth is higher than normal, incomes of consumers tend to rise, and consumers spend more money. This results in higher sales revenue for firms.

1.2 Weak Economic Growth
Weak economy results in lower incomes, a reduction in consumer spending, and a reduction in business sales.

1.3 Indicators of Economic Growth
- Growth in GDP
- Level of unemployment
    - Frictional unemployment — people are temporarily between jobs
    - Seasonal unemployment — people whose services are not needed during some seasons
    - Cyclical unemployment — people who cannot find employment because firms are not hiring, due to poor economic conditions
    - Structural unemployment — people who lack the skills needed by firms

Of the four types of unemployment, cyclical unemployment is probably the best indicator of economic conditions.

2. Impact of Inflation

Inflation is the increase in the general level of prices of goods and services over a specified period of time.

2.1 Types of Inflation
- Cost-push inflation — results from higher costs of production. Some firms rely heavily on oil or other resources that are subject to major price increases.
- Demand-pull inflation — results from strong consumer demand for goods and services, which allows firms to raise prices.

3. Impact of Interest Rates

3.1 Impact on a Firm's Expenses

3.2 Impact on a Firm's Expansion

3.3 Impact on a Firm's Revenue

3.4 How Rising Interest Rates Affected the Housing Crisis

4. Market Prices Are Determined

4.1 Demand Schedule for a Product
Indicates the quantity of a product that would be demanded at each possible price.

4.2 Supply Schedule for a Product
Indicates the quantity of a product that firms would be willing and able to supply at each possible price.

4.3 Interaction of Demand and Supply
- If the price is too is high, the quantity supplied exceeds the quantity demanded, resulting in a surplus.
- If the price is too low, the quantity demanded exceeds the quantity supplied, resulting in a shortage.
- The price at which the quantity supplied is equal to the quantity demanded is the equilibrium price.

4.4 Effect of a Change in the Demand Schedule
When the demand increases, the equilibrium price rises. When demand falls, the equilibrium price declines.

4.5 Effect of a Change in the Supply Schedule
When supply increases, the equilibrium price will fall. When supply decreases, the equilibrium price will rise.

4.6 Effect of Demand and Supply on the General Price Level
When aggregate demand increases, the price level for products in general rises. When aggregate supply decreases, the price level could also increase.

4.7 How Consumer Income Affects Market Prices
An increase in income results in a higher consumer demand.

4.8 Consumer Preferences
A shift in preferences results in higher demand for some products, and lower demand for other products.

4.9 Production Expenses
Higher expenses cause firms to raise the prices of their products, while lower expenses allow firms to lower prices.

5. Government Influence On Economic Conditions

5.1 Monetary Policy
- The U.S. money supply is defined as the sum of demand deposits (funds in checking accounts), currency (coins and paper money) held by the public, and traveler's checks. Monetary policy represents the actions of the Fed to control the money supply.
- The Fed reduces interest rates by increasing the amount of funds in the banking system. Lower interest rates can stimulate economic growth.
- The Fed increases interest rates by reducing the amount of funds in the banking system. Higher interest rates can reduce economic growth and inflation.

5.2 Fiscal Policy
Fiscal policy involves decisions by the federal government about how it should set tax rates and spend money.
- Revision of corporate taxes affects a firm's after-tax earnings (profits) directly.
- Revision of excise taxes (on specific products) affects consumer spending on specific products.
- The federal budget deficit is the amount by which federal spending exceeds federal tax revenue.
- Lower tax rates and an increase in government spending can increase economic growth and the demand for goods and services. But it also increases the federal budget deficit.

5.3 Summary of Government Influence on the Economy

Lower tax rates give consumers more after-tax income and can increase spending. Higher tax rates reduces after-tax income and spending.

5.4 Dilemma of the Federal Government

- The federal government can reduce inflation by using a restrictive monetary policy and by raising taxes. However, restrictive monetary and fiscal policies may cause economic growth to slow down and the unemployment rate to rise.
- The federal government can reduce unemployment by using expansionary monetary and fiscal policies. However, these policies may increase inflation.

Solutions to End-of-Chapter Exercises

Concept Review Questions

(1) Impact of Economy on Business Value. Explain why the value of a business is affected by economic conditions.

High growth enhances demand for products because the total income level earned by consumers who have jobs is relatively high. Thus, there is a higher volume of spending on products and services, which results in higher revenue, higher profits, and a higher value of the business. However, slow economic growth results in lower demand for products and a reduction in a firm's revenue and value.

(2) Impact of Inflation. Explain why the value of a business is influenced by inflation.

Inflation results in higher expenses to the firm when it purchases supplies or develops production facilities. It also may force the firm to pay higher salaries. If the firm cannot easily pass these higher costs on to consumers with higher pricing, it will suffer a reduction in profits and in the value of its business.

(3) Unemployment. Describe the four different types of unemployment. Which type is the best indicator of a possible weak economy?

Frictional unemployment represents people who are between jobs. Seasonal unemployment represents people whose services are needed on a seasonal basis. Cyclical unemployment refers to people who cannot find jobs because of poor economic conditions. Structural unemployment represents people who cannot find jobs because they lack adequate work skills.

(4) Inflation. Explain the difference between cost-push inflation and demand-pull inflation.

Cost-push inflation results when firms increase the prices they charge for their products in response to higher production expenses. Demand-pull inflation results from firms increasing their prices of products and services in response to an increase in demand. Cost-push inflation can occur even when economic conditions are weak, while demand-pull inflation normally occurs when there is a strong economy.

(5) Inflation. Why are businesses affected by inflation?

A high rate of inflation can influence the performance of firms because it affects the production expenses or cost of supplies and materials incurred by firms. This may reduce the profits of businesses.

(6) Interest Rates. Explain how interest rate movements affect the performance of a business.

Interest rates determine the cost of borrowing funds. When interest rates rise, businesses incur higher borrowing costs. In addition, if they sell products on credit, their customers incur higher costs of credit and may reduce their demand for the products produced by businesses.

(7) Product Shortage. Explain how demand and supply conditions can cause a shortage to occur. What happens to the price in response to a shortage?

For a given market price, the demand could exceed supply, causing a shortage. Firms can raise their price and supply more of the product, while the quantity demanded by consumers declines in response to the higher price. This eliminates the shortage.

(8) Price Level. Explain the effect of demand and supply on the general price level in the economy.

If the aggregate (total) demand for products by consumers increases, this will pull up the general level of prices. If the supply schedule of all or most products suddenly decreases (perhaps because of higher oil prices or other factors that can increase production costs), the general level of prices should rise.

(9) Monetary Policy. Explain how monetary policy can affect the performance of businesses.

Monetary policy determines the money supply and level of interest rates. If the Federal Reserve reduces interest rates, it reduces the firm's cost of borrowing. Lower interest rates also reduce the cost of credit to consumers and encourage more spending (more demand for products) by consumers.

(10) Monetary and Fiscal Policies. Explain the difference between monetary policy and fiscal policy.

Monetary policy is implemented by the Federal Reserve System. The Fed adjusts interest rates by adjusting the amount of funds in the banking system. Changes in interest rates influence the demand for a firm's products that are purchased with the use of consumer credit. In addition, changes in interest rates affect the interest expenses incurred by the firm. Fiscal policy involves decisions regarding tax rates and the level of government spending. A change in personal income tax rates affects the amount of money that consumers have to spend. A change in the level of government spending affects the aggregate demand for products and services.

Class Communication Questions

(1) Impact of Demand-Pull Versus Cost-Push Inflation on Your Business. As a business owner, would you prefer a situation in which there is demand-pull inflation or cost-push inflation?

Demand-pull inflation allows you to raise prices even if your production expenses have not increased, so you may be able to increase your profits. Conversely, cost-push inflation reflects the raising of prices in response to higher expenses, so your profits will not necessarily increase. Therefore, demand-pull inflation is more desirable from the perspective of a business owner.

(2) Impact of the Fed on Businesses. Assume that the U.S. economy is currently weak, and the Fed wants to enact a monetary policy that will lower interest rates in order to stimulate the economy. However, this policy could cause higher inflation. Alternatively, the Fed could leave interest rates at their present level and avoid the danger of higher inflation. Do you think businesses would be better off in this case if the Fed lowered interest rates?

Lower interest rates can reduce a firm's expense from borrowing funds. In addition, lower rates could reduce the cost of borrowing for consumers, which can increase consumer demand for products. Yet, the higher consumer demand could cause demand-pull inflation. Even if lower interest rates result in higher inflation, most businesses would prefer that situation to a weak economy. However, the answer may depend on how high inflation rises.

(3) Budget Deficit Dilemma. Assume that the U.S. unemployment rate is high. The U.S. government could use a fiscal policy to stimulate the economy by reducing personal tax rates. This policy will be beneficial because it provides consumers with more money to spend. However, the federal government will receive less tax revenue and will therefore experience a larger federal budget deficit. Is it appropriate for the government to go into more debt every time that it wants to stimulate the economy?

Many businesses would be glad that the government is enacting a fiscal policy that will stimulate the economy, but this could cause problems for the United States in the long run. If the government borrows excessively over time, there may be a point at which it has difficult borrowing money because of questions about its ability to repay the debt. However, most people and businesses would likely prefer a quick solution to a slow economy even if there might be adverse long-term consequences.

Small Business Case — Managing in Response to Economic Conditions

Prestige Tile Company specializes in the production of fancy tile that it installs in the lobbies of hotels, banks, restaurants, and other companies. The economy has been strong, so the businesses that it serves have been experiencing high profits and have been able to afford the services of Prestige Tile. However, the production plant that it rents is currently at full capacity.

(1) Responding to Economic Growth. As a result of recent economic growth, Prestige Tile is considering the purchase of a very large production plant and hiring more full-time employees so that it can produce a larger volume of tile. What is the risk of investing substantial funds to expand the plant and hiring new employees?

> If the economy weakens, the demand for its tile will likely decline. Thus, it may not need the extra plant space or the extra employees. There is risk that it could waste a substantial amount of money in expansion that will not necessarily lead to more sales.

(2) Impact of Inflation on Business Expenses. Prestige Tile Company incurs expenses in the form of purchases of materials, rent payments for its production plant, utility expenses to run the production, and salaries paid to employees. Explain why an increase in inflation could affect its expenses and profits.

> If inflation rises, the cost of materials, rent, utilities, and salaries may increase. Thus, its expenses will increase, and this may reduce its profits.

(3) Impact of Interest Rates on Business Expenses. Prestige Tile Company relies on short-term loans to support some of its operations. Explain how its expenses and profits may be affected by an increase in interest rates.

> When interest rates rise, it pays higher interest rates on the funds that it borrowed. Therefore, its overall expenses increase, and its profits are reduced.

(4) Impact of Monetary Policy on Business Expenses. The Federal Reserve is planning to increase interest rates in order to slow economic growth because it believes the economy is too strong and will cause higher inflation if it continues to grow so fast. Explain how the Fed's policy might affect the expenses and profits of Prestige Tile Company.

> If the Fed raises interest rates, the cost of borrowing will increase, and the firm will have higher expenses and lower profits.

Web Insight — Exposure of Harley-Davidson to Economic Conditions

At the opening of the chapter, Harley-Davidson was introduced. Go to its website (www.harley-davidson.com) and go to the section called "Investor Relations." Summarize Harley-Davidson's stock price performance during the last quarter or year. Does it appear that its performance has been influenced by economic conditions during the last quarter or year? (You can also learn about its recent performance by reviewing the Letter to Shareholders, which is near the beginning of its annual report.)

The stock price performance changes over time and normally is sensitive to economic conditions. It performs better when economic conditions are favorable.

Dell's Secret for Success

Go to Dell's website (www.dell.com) and click on the link "About Dell," near the bottom of the web page. Review the information about Dell's recent performance. You can also review a recent annual report of Dell for more information.

(1) Exposure to Economy. Describe Dell's recent business performance. Do you think that Dell's business performance was sensitive to the economy? Explain.

Like most firms, Dell's business tends to be more favorable when the economy is strong. Dell tends to generate strong sales even when economic conditions are weak. This is because some of Dell's products are viewed almost like necessities.

(2) Comparison of Product Exposure. During a weak economy, the demand for some of Dell's products may decline. Which products would likely experience a decline in demand?

The products that are not needed (perhaps more expensive computers) may be subject to a decline in sales when the economy is weak.

(3) Impact of Interest Rates. If interest rates increase, why might the demand for Dell's products be affected?

Higher interest rates increase the cost of borrowing and may reduce the consumer demand for Dell's products that were to be purchased with borrowed money.

Video Exercise — Lessons in How Economic Conditions Affect Businesses

Many free business videos are available on websites such as YouTube (www.youtube.com), and more are added every day. Search for a recent video clip about an existing business that offers lessons on "U.S. economy" in YouTube or any other website that provides video clips.

(1) Main Lesson. Is the video clip focused on interest rates, economic growth, unemployment, inflation, or some other aspect of the economy? What is the main lesson of the video clip that you watched?

Answers will vary among students. The main point is to ensure that students take the initiative to access and watch a related video, and recognize the main lesson provided by the video.

(2) Adapting to Changes. Many related videos suggest that a key lesson for entrepreneurs is to be ready to adapt to changes in the business environment. How do you think a business can stay more "flexible" in order to adapt to changing economic conditions?

A new business should allow for the possibility that economic conditions will be worse than expected, which could result in lower sales and revenue. Thus, it might need access to additional financing in order to cover its expenses. If the economic conditions are better than expected, it could sell more products than it expected, but it needs a way to quickly increase its production to satisfy a higher level of demand.

(3) Impact of Interest Rate Movements. An important lesson is how a change in the interest rate affects the amount of interest expenses incurred by the business and its ability to repay its loans. Explain why some businesses experience problems when interest rates rise.

When interest rates rise, the interest owed on business loans tends to rise. Thus, the interest expenses rise, and firms may have difficult covering their interest payments.

Chapter 4: Assessing Global Conditions

Introduction

The **Learning Objectives** for this chapter are to:

1. Explain the motives for U.S. firms to engage in international business.

2. Describe how firms conduct international business.

3. Explain how barriers to international business have been reduced and describe the barriers that remain.

4. Explain how foreign characteristics can influence a firm's international business.

5. Explain how exchange rate movements can affect a firm's performance.

1. How International Business Can Enhance Performance

1.1 Attract Foreign Demand — where there is high profit potential in foreign markets.

1.2 Capitalize on Technology — advantages that U.S. firms can apply compared to firms based in less-developed countries.

1.3 Use Inexpensive Resources — pursue countries with low labor and land costs.

1.4 Diversify Internationally — U.S. firms can reduce their exposure to U.S. economy by sellling their products in various countries.

1.5 Combination of Motives

2. How Firms Conduct International Business

2.1 Importing involves the purchase of foreign products or services.
- Tariff — tax on imported products
- Quota — limits the amount of a specific product that can be imported

2.2 Exporting — the sale of products or services (called exports) to purchasers residing in other countries.

2.3 Direct Foreign Investment (DFI) — acquiring or establishing facilities in a foreign county.

2.4 Outsourcing — of services to foreign countries to use cheaper labor.

2.5 Strategic Alliances — agreements with foreign firms to pursue mutual interests.

3. **Barriers to International Business**
   - Any government may impose barriers to protect its own firms.
   - Trade barriers are sometimes used to punish countries for actions such as not enforcing environmental or child labor laws.

3.1 Reduction in Barriers
   - North American Free Trade Agreement (NAFTA) of 1993 — eliminated trade barriers between the United States, Mexico, and Canada.
   - General Agreement on Tariffs and Trade (GATT) — reduced or eliminated trade restrictions on specified imported products across 117 countries.
   - In June 2003, The United States and Chile signed a free trade agreement to remove tariffs on more than 90% of products that are sent between the United States and Latin American countries.
   - Over time, countries in Europe have eliminated many trade barriers.

3.2 Remaining Barriers

3.3 Disagreements About Trade Barriers
Use the following examples to ignite discussion about how these disagreements should be resolved.
   - Firms based in one country are not subject to environmental restrictions and can produce at lower costs than those in other countries.
   - Firms based in one country are not subject to labor laws and can use children as labor, keeping costs low.
   - Firms based in one country are allowed by their governement to offer bribes to large customers when pursuing deals, giving them an advantage.
   - Firms in one country receive tax breaks if they are in specific industries.

4. **How Foreign Characteristics Influence International Business**

4.1 Culture
A firm must learn a foreign country's **culture** before it engages in business there. Poor decisions can result from an improper assessment of a foreign country's tastes, habits, and customs.

4.2 Economic System

A country's **economic system** will indicate the degree of government ownership of businesses and intervention in business.

- **Capitalism** allows for private ownership of all businesses. Entrepreneurs are allowed to create businesses that they believe will serve the people's needs.
- **Communism** is an economic system that involves public ownership of businesses. The government decides what products consumers will be offered and in what quantities.
- **Socialism** contains some features of both capitalism and communism. Socialist governments allow people to own businesses and property and to select their own jobs. However, these governments provide a variety of public services, such as generous unemployment benefits, which are paid by high tax rates on income. Entrepreneurs will have less incentive to establish businesses if the tax rates are excessively high.
- **Privatization** is the selling of government-owned businesses to private investors. This allows some governments to convert to a more capialistic system, and it allows U.S. firms to own businesses in foreign countries that previously prohibited U.S. investment.

4.3 Economic Conditions

- Economic growth in a foreign country affects consumer demand for products.
- Inflation in a foreign country can affect a firm's cost of materials and production there.

4.4 Exchange Rates

If the U.S. dollar weakens (depreciates), a U.S. firm will need more dollars to purchase a given amount of foreign supplies, but foreign firms can purchase U.S. products at a relatively low price. If the U.S. dollar strengthens, a U.S. firm can purchase materials at a relatively low price, but foreign firms would be discouraged from buying U.S. products because the dollar is too expensive.

4.5 Political Risk and Regulations

Political risk is the risk that a country's political actions may adversely affect a business. Corruption and government regulations are components of political risk.

5. How Exchange Rate Movements Can Affect Performance

5.1 Impact of a Weak Dollar on U.S. Importers — increases the cost

5.2 Impact of a Strong Dollar on U.S. Importers — reduces the cost

5.3 Actual Effects of Exchange Rate Movements on U.S. Importers

5.4 Impact of a Weak Dollar on U.S. Exporters — U.S. products can be purchased with a smaller amount of foreign currency, so demand is high.

5.5 Impact of a Strong Dollar on U.S. Exporters — U.S. products are expensive to foreign purchasers so demand for U.S. exports is low.

5.6 Hedging Against Exchange Rate Movements
- Hedging payments for imports — use a **forward contract** to buy foreign currency at a specified exchange rate at a specified future point in time. The exchange rate that the contract provides is referred to as the **forward rate**.
- Hedging receivables — use a **forward contract** to buy foreign currency at a specified exchange rate at a specified future point in time. The exchange rate that the contract provides is referred to as the **forward rate**.

5.7 How Exchange Rates Affect Foreign Competition — strong dollar encourages U.S. consumers to buy foreign products instead of U.S.-produced products.

Solutions to End-of-Chapter Exercises

Concept Review Questions

(1) International Business Motives. Explain why a U.S. firm is motivated to pursue international business.

A business may pursue international business in order to:

- Attract foreign demand — where there is high profit potential in foreign markets.

- Capitalize on technology — advantages that U.S. firms can apply compared to firms based in less-developed countries.

- Use inexpensive resources — move operations to countries with low labor and land costs.

- Diversify internationally — U.S. firms can reduce the exposure to U.S. economy by sellling their products in various countries.

(2) Trade Barriers. Explain the difference between a tariff and a quota. Explain why these international trade barriers protect a local firm's business from foreign competition.

A tariff is a tax on imported products, while a quota limits the amount of a specific product that can be imported. These barriers discourage or prevent imports, which forces local consumers to rely on local products.

(3) Exporting Versus Importing. What is the difference between exporting and importing?

Exporting involves selling a product or service to customers in a foreign country, while importing involves buying a product or service from a foreign firm located in another country.

(4) International Business Methods. Describe common methods used to conduct international business.

Methods include:

- **Importing** which involves the purchase of foreign products or services.

- **Exporting** which is the sale of products or services (called exports) to purchasers residing in other countries.

- **Direct foreign investment (DFI)** which involves acquiring or establishing facilities in a foreign country.

- **Outsourcing** of services to foreign countries to use cheaper labor.

- **Strategic alliances** which are agreements with foreign firms to pursue mutual interests.

(5) China's Advantage. What is the major reason why U.S. consumers desire products that are produced in China and other Asian countries?

The cost of labor in China is very low, which allows Chinese firms to charge very low prices for their products.

(6) Direct Foreign Investment. Explain why U.S. firms may pursue direct foreign investment (DFI).

Direct foreign investment (DFI) represents the act of acquiring or building subsidiaries in one or more foreign countries. It is commonly used to capitalize on low-cost labor or to capitalize on technology. It may reduce the transportation costs of exporting or may even circumvent a foreign government's trade barrier.

(7) Strategic Alliance. Why might a firm pursue a strategic alliance rather than direct foreign investment?

A firm engages in direct foreign investment when it acquires or builds subsidiaries in one or more foreign countries. This is very expensive. An alternative approach is to engage in a strategic alliance with a foreign business, which may involve profit sharing between the two parties. The firm can avoid a large investment with a strategic alliance.

(8) Economic Systems. Explain the different types of economic systems that may be found among countries.

A country's economic system reflects the degree of government ownership of businesses and intervention in business. **Capitalism** allows for private ownership of all businesses. Entrepreneurs are allowed to create businesses that they believe will serve the people's needs. **Communism** is an economic system that involves public ownership of businesses. The government decides what products consumers will be offered and in what quantities. **Socialism** contains some features of both capitalism and communism. Socialist governments allow people to own businesses and property and to select their own jobs. However, these governments provide a variety of public services, such as generous unemployment benefits, which are paid by high tax rates on income.

(9) Foreign Economic Conditions. Explain why a firm's sales to customers in a foreign country may be highly influenced by the foreign country's economic conditions.

The income levels of foreign consumers is based on the economic growth in that country. The demand by foreign customers for products is dependent on their income level.

(10) Weak Dollar Effect. Explain how a weak dollar affects the performance of U.S. firms that attempt to export their products.

A weak dollar allows foreign customers to buy U.S. products at a low price. This results in a strong demand for U.S. products, which is beneficial to U.S. firms.

Class Communication Questions

(1) Imposing Barriers on Imports from China. U.S. imports from China exceed U.S. exports to China by more than $150 billion each year. Many U.S. businesses want the U.S. government to place barriers on imports from China because they believe that China has an unfair advantage (they allege that China uses children in factories). However, if the U.S. government places barriers on the imports, U.S. consumers would have to pay a higher price for many products. Should the U.S. government impose barriers on China?

If China is using children as labor, it may have an unfair cost advantage, and this is a human rights issue. But many exporters based in China do not rely on children for labor, so these firms should not be punished. In general, China's labor expenses are much lower than labor expenses in the United States, and that is why its products can be priced lower than U.S. products. Some U.S. businesses capitalize on the low labor cost in China by importing supplies or materials from there.

(2) Outsource Decision. You want to start a business in the United States. You would outsource some of the work to Mexico, because you can achieve low labor costs, and this would be necessary for your business to survive. Some critics may suggest that to reduce the U.S.

unemployment rate, you should hire people in the United States rather than outsource. What is your opinion?

While you may wish you could help reduce the level of U.S. unemployment, hiring people in the United States would cause your expenses to be too high and you might go bankrupt. If you were required to hire employees in the United States, you would not create your business.

(3) Foreign Competition. Do you think foreign competitors have an unfair advantage over U.S. firms?

Some students may think that foreign firms are subsidized by their governments more than U.S. firms are subsidized by the U.S. government. Others may argue that U.S. firms use lack of subsidies as an excuse. It is difficult to compare government subsidies across countries because there are many different ways to subsidize firms, including lower corporate tax rates.

Small Business Case — Managing in Response to Global Conditions

Victory Company produces computer games and sells them in the United States. Its major concern is the high cost of producing the computer chips that it uses for the computer games. It contacts a supplier of chips in China and describes the types of chips that it needs. The supplier offers to produce the chips and sell them to Victory Company for a price that is 30 percent lower than its cost of production and is much lower than U.S. chip manufacturers charge. By relying on chips made in China, it can reduce its expenses and charge a lower price for its computer games. This will likely result in a much higher demand for its games, and its revenue and profits should increase.

(1) Reason for Reliance on Foreign Materials. Why do you think that China is able to produce chips at a lower cost than the U.S. firms?

China's wages are substantially lower than wages in the United States.

(2) Impact of Reliance on Foreign Materials. When Victory Company relies on a foreign manufacturer to produce the chips rather than producing the chips itself, what do you think will happen to its employees who produced the chips in the past?

The employees will likely be laid off unless the firm has some open job positions that can be filled with the employees who used to produce the chips.

(3) Impact of a Tariff on Businesses. If Victory Company decides to import computer chips, and the U.S. government imposes a tariff on imports from China, how would this affect the overall expenses incurred by Victory?

The cost of the imported chips and the expenses of the firm would increase if a tariff is imposed.

(4) Impact of Exchange Rate Movements. If Victory Company decides to import computer chips, and the price is denominated in Chinese currency (called the yuan), how will the cost of the imports to Victory Company change if the yuan appreciates over time against the dollar?

If the Chinese yuan appreciates against the dollar, the cost of the imported chips would increase and the expenses of Victory Company would increase.

Web Insight — Nike's International Business

At the opening of the chapter, Nike Inc. was introduced. Go to the website (www.nikebiz.com /company_overview). Summarize the comments made about Nike's international business.

Nike has substantial international business. It has grown internationally to capitalize on new markets and also benefits from a low cost of production in some Asian countries.

Dell's Secret for Success

Go to Dell's website (http://www.dell.com) and click on the link "About Dell," near the bottom of the web page. Review the section that describes Dell's international business. You can also review a recent annual report of Dell for more information.

(1) International Business. Describe Dell's business in international markets.

Dell has grown in Europe and Asia (including China).

(2) Direct Foreign Investment. What do you think motivated Dell to pursue direct foreign investment in international markets?

It produces products that would be in demand in these markets. In addition, some of these markets have low-cost labor, which it can use to produce its products.

(3) Expansion in Asia. Why do you think some Asian countries could appeal to Dell even if the demand for computers in those countries is low?

Some of these markets have low cost labor, where it can have it products produced.

Video Exercise — Lessons in How Global Conditions Affect a Business

Many free business videos are available on websites such as YouTube (www.youtube.com), and more are added every day. Search for a recent video clip about an existing business that offers lessons on "company international business" in YouTube or any other website that provides video clips.

(1) Main Lesson. Is the video clip focused on the potential impact of different cultures in the international environment, different regulations, exchange rate effects, or some other global factor that affects a business? What is the main lesson of the video clip that you watched?

Answers will vary among students. The main point is to ensure that students take the initiative to access and watch a related video and recognize the main lesson provided by the video.

(2) Adapting to a Culture. A common lesson in many business video clips is that a business must adjust its products or services to fit the culture of the host country. Explain how a firm's international business performance may be dependent on whether it adjusts its products or services to fit the culture of the host country.

If a business does not adjust its products or services, it may not satisfy the customers in the foreign country. Thus, its sales will suffer, and its performance will suffer as a result.

(3) Impact of Changing Exchange Rates. U.S. businesses commonly experience a reduction in international business when foreign currencies weaken against the dollar. Furthermore, exchange rate movements are difficult to forecast accurately. What is the lesson here for a U.S. business entrepreneur who is planning expansion in another country and is attempting to forecast revenue from sales in that country?

The lesson is to consider various possible exchange rate scenarios that may occur, since the actual sales level will probably be dependent on the prevailing exchange rates.

Solutions to End-of-Part Exercises (Part I)

Video on Managing a Business — It Takes Money to Make Money

The Small Business Administration (SBA) plays a very important role in helping many small businesses. Its website, which offers a wide range of services and information for small businesses, has a section called Delivering Success (www.sba.gov/tools/audiovideo/ deliveringsuccess/index.html) that provides video clips of small business success stories. Go to this website, and watch the video called "Getting Started" (total time of clip is 3 minutes, 45 seconds).

In this video clip, two entrepreneurs explain their success. One of the key points is that it takes money to make money. Entrepreneurs commonly need funding in order to achieve their business plans. The SBA helps many entrepreneurs obtain financing by providing a guarantee to commercial banks that the loan will be repaid. That is, if the small business does not repay the loan, the SBA will cover the loan. Since the bank does not have to worry about the risk of loan default, it is more willing to provide loans to small businesses.

(1) Interaction Between Financing and Corporate Responsibilities. As entrepreneurs obtain financing, their priority is to cover their financing and other expenses so that they can continue their business. Does this mean that their focus on maximizing their value (Chapter 1) requires them to ignore corporate responsibilities (Chapter 2)?

Ultimately, firms are responsible for repaying their creditors and satisfying their owners. They incur costs from satisfying their corporate responsibilities. However, as they spend money to satisfy their corporate responsibilities, they can also benefit because they can more easily retain customers and employees.

(2) Interaction Between Financing and Economic Exposure. Explain how the financing decision (amount of debt financing versus equity financing) of a small business (Chapter 1) affects its exposure to economic conditions (Chapter 3). That is, would a firm that obtains mostly debt financing from a bank or equity financing from other investors be more likely to fail if a recession occurred? Why?

A firm that relied on debt would be more likely to fail because it would have to make debt payments to repay the loan. Conversely, it would not have to make any payments to investors who provided equity funding. Yet, entrepreneurs must give up part of their ownership to these investors, and that is why they may prefer to rely on loans from banks instead of equity financing from investors.

(3) Interaction Between Financing and International Business. Explain how the financing decision (amount of debt financing versus equity financing) of a small business (Chapter 1) affects its ability to pursue international business (Chapter 4). That is, would a firm that obtains mostly debt financing from a bank or equity financing from other investors be more likely to expand into a foreign country? Why?

A firm that relied on equity would be more likely to engage in international business because it would not have to use any of its revenue received to pay off debt. It would have more money available to reinvest in the firm after paying general expenses (such as salaries to employees).

Chapter 5: Selecting a Form of Business Ownership

Introduction

The **Learning Objectives** for this chapter are to:

1. Describe the advantages and disadvantages of a sole proprietorship.

2. Describe the advantages and disadvantages of a partnership.

3. Describe the advantages and disadvantages of a corporation.

4. Explain how the potential return and risk of a business are affected by its form of ownership.

5. Describe methods of owning existing businesses.

1. Sole Proprietorship

A **sole proprietorship** is a business owned by a single owner. The owner is called the sole proprietor. About 70 percent of all firms are sole proprietorships.

1.1 Characteristics of Successful Sole Proprietors — willing to accept risk, willing to work long hours, have good management skills, have experience in industry.

1.2 Advantages of a Sole Proprietorship
- All earnings go to the sole proprietor
- Easy organization
- Complete control
- Lower taxes

1.3 Disadvantages of a Sole Proprietorship
- Sole proprietor also incurs all losses
- Unlimited liability
- Limited access to funds
- Sole proprietors may have limited skills

2. Partnership

A **partnership** is a business that is co-owned by two or more people. The owners of the business are called partners. About 10 percent of all firms are organized as partnerships.

In a **general partnership**, all partners have unlimited liability. In a **limited partnership**, some of the partners have limited liability.

2.1 General Versus Limited Partnership

2.2 Advantages of a Partnership
- Additional funding — more owners can result in more funding
- Shared losses — any losses are absorbed by more than one owner
- Ability to specialize — partners can focus on areas of specialization

2.3 Disadvantages of a Partnership
- Shared control — owners might disagree about business decisions
- Unlimited liability — all general partners have unlimited liability
- Shared profits — profits must be shared among partners

2.4. S-Corporation
Some small firms with 100 or fewer owners that satisfy certain criteria can avoid the problem of unlimited liability by forming an **S-corporation**.

2.5. Limited LiabilityCompany (LLC)
A **limited liability company (LLC)** has the regular features of a general partnership, but also offers limited liability by protecting a partner's personal assets from the negligence of other partners.

3. Corporation
A **corporation** is a state-chartered business entity that pays taxes and is legally distinct from its owners.About 20 percent of all firms are corporations, and these corporations generate almost 90 percent of all business revenue.

3.1 Charter and Bylaws
The owners of a corporation are called **shareholders**. Since the corporation is legally distinct from its owners, shareholders have limited liability for the debts of the company. The shareholders elect a **board of directors**, who are then responsible for establishing the general policies of the corporation and appointing the president and other key officers of the corporation.

3.2 How Stockholders Earn a Return
- Dividends — portion of the firm's recent earnings paid to the stockholders
- Capital gain — increase in the market value of the stock over time

3.3 Private Versus Public Corporations

3.4 Advantages of a Corporation
- Limited liability — unlike sole proprietors or general partners in a partnership, shareholders of corporations have limited liability
- Easier access to funds — the ability to issue additional stock provides corporations with a means of raising additional funds that is not available to sole proprietorships and partnerships
- Transfer of ownership — stockholders in publicly held corporations can normally sell their stock by simply calling a stockbroker. Owners of sole proprietorships and partnerships may have a difficult time selling their business interests

3.5 Disadvantages of a Corporation
- **Additional organizational expense** — a corporation must create a corporate charter and file it with the state government
- **Financial disclosure** — publicly held corporations must disclose more about their operations and financial condition
- **Agency problems** — publicly held corporations are normally run by professional managers, who may make decisions that conflict with the interests of owners
- **High taxes** — earnings of the corporation are first taxed as income to the corporation. If the corporation pays dividends to stockholders, the dividends are taxed again as the personal income of the owners of the corporation.

3.6 Comparing Forms of Business Ownership — compare advantages and disadvantages

3.7 How Business Ownership Can Change

4. How Ownership Can Affect Return and Risk
The potential **return** and **risk** from investing in a business are influenced by the form of ownership.

4.1 Impact of Ownership on the Return on Investment
Return on equity (ROE) is lower for a firm that uses more equity unless it invests its equity funds in a manner that will increase its net income substantially.

4.2 Impact of Ownership on Risk
Risk refers to the degree of uncertainty about the firm's future earnings. Earnings are the difference between revenue and expenses, so lower-than-expected revenue or higher-than-expected expenses (or both) could cause a firm to experience losses. Owners can reduce their risk by allowing investors to have part of the ownership, but then they must share profits.

5. Obtaining Ownership of an Existing Business

5.1 Assuming Ownership of a Family Business — owner is already familiar with the business

5.2 Purchasing an Existing Business

5.3 Franchising — an arrangement whereby a business owner (called the franchisor) allows others (called franchisees) to use its trademark, trade name, or copyright, under specified conditions

Types of franchises include a distributorship, in which a firm is allowed to sell a product produced by a manufacturer; a chain-style business, which is allowed to use the trade name of a company and follows guidelines related to the pricing and sale of the product; and a **manufacturing arrangement,** which allows a firm to manufacture a product using formulas or methods provided by another company.

- Advantages of franchises — proven management style, name recognition, and financial support
- Disadvantages of franchises — shared profits and less control (franchisee must agree to guidelines set by the franchisor)

Solutions to End-of-Chapter Exercises

Concept Review Questions

(1) Forms of Business Ownership. Compare and contrast a sole proprietorship, a partnership, and a corporation.

A sole proprietorship is a firm owned and usually managed by a single person. The single owner receives all profits but also incurs all losses and has unlimited liability. A partnership consists of two or more owners who must share profits, but also share losses. A corporation is a business entity that legally is considered to be separate from its owners, which means that owners have limited liability. Owners (stockholders) allow management to run the business

(2) Advantages of a Sole Proprietorship. Why is the sole proprietorship such a popular form of business.

The owner does not have to share earnings of the business, the business is easy to organize, the owner has complete control, and taxes may be lower.

(3) Advantage of a Limited Partnership. Explain why owners may establish a limited partnership instead of a general partnership.

In a general partnership, all partners have unlimited liability. Owners may want to attract more funds but without allowing any new partners to have control in the decisions. So they can create a limited partnership to allow for limited partners.

(4) Advantage of an LLC. What is a limited liability company (LLC), and why is it so popular?

A limited liability company allows limited liability for the partners by protecting a partner's personal assets from the negligence of other partners in the firm.

(5) Return to Stockholders. How can stockholders earn a return on their investment?

Stockholders may receive dividends from the firm, which are a portion of the firm's recent earnings. In addition, the stock value may increase over time and generate a capital gain for the stockholders when they sell the stock.

(6) Private Versus Public Firms. Distinguish between privately held and publicly held corporations.

A privately held corporation is owned by a small group of investors. A publicly held firm issues stock to anyone who wants to purchase it. These investors can sell their holdings of the stock at any time over an organized stock exchange at the prevailing market price at that time. Publicly held corporations can obtain additional financing by issuing additional shares of stock.

(7) Motive for Going Public. Why might a business want to become a publicly held corporation?

A publicly held corporation has easy access to funds because it can issue more shares when it needs funds. Thus, it can easily expand its business. Its owners have limited liability. Ownership of the stock can be easily transferred.

(8) Concern About Going Public. Why would a partnership worry about the possible mismanagement of its business if it converted to a publicly held corporation?

As the business expands into a publicly held corporation, managers will be hired to manage the firm. These managers are supposed to make decisions that are in the best interests of the owners, but sometimes they make decisions that are in their own interests. Consequently, the performance of the firm may decline.

(9) Advantages of a Franchise. Describe a franchise and explain why an entrepreneur may prefer to obtain ownership of a business through franchising.

Franchises offer a proven management style, name recognition, and sometimes financial support.

(10) Types of Franchises. Identify the common types of franchises and explain each type.

The types of franchises are:
- **Distributorship** — an arrangement in which a firm is allowed to sell a product produced by a manufacturer.
- **Chain-style business** — allowed to use the trade name of a company and follows guidelines related to the pricing and sale of the product.
- **Manufacturing arrangement** — allows a firm to manufacture a product using formulas or methods provided by another company.

Class Communication Questions

(1) Proprietorship Versus Partnership. You own a proprietorship that is successful. You would like to expand your business but are constrained because you cannot obtain more loans. You have a very good friend who would provide your business with funding if he is allowed to be a part-owner. However, he does not understand your business and would not be helpful in running your business. Should you allow him to be a part-owner in order to obtain more funding?

You could allow him to be a limited partner. He would provides funding and share in the profits of your business, but would not be involved in the management of your business.

(2) Franchise Decision. You have an opportunity to buy a small restaurant franchise, which is part of a popular chain in your city. Alternatively, you could start your own restaurant business and would have more control regarding how to run the restaurant. Which investment would be less risky?

The franchise would probably be less risky because it already has proved itself in your city. There is more uncertainty surrounding the performance of a new restaurant.

(3) Ownership of a Corporation. You are aware of a company that is going public by selling 10 million shares of stock. You consider purchasing 300 shares of the stock. The company suggests that as a shareholder, you can influence its business decisions. Do you agree?

You would have a very small proportion of the ownership. You would be allowed to vote on some issues that allow shareholders to vote, but you would not have sufficient ownership to influence the business decisions.

Small Business Case — Deciding the Type of Business Ownership

Dave Books and Kevin Warden have decided to start a partnership in which they create a video that provides golf lessons. Dave has $30,000 to invest. He plans to run the business on his own but needs additional funding. Kevin Warden has agreed to invest $30,000 in this business. Dave will produce the video and attempt to sell it directly to customers through a website that they will create. Dave will manage the business, while Kevin's main role will be to invest funds to support the business. The business is expected to earn net income of about $10,000 in the first year. If Dave expands the business over time, he will allow other investors to invest funds, but he will manage the business on his own.

(1) Business Ownership. What form of business ownership would you recommend for this business?

This business should be set up as a limited partnership form of business ownership and control. Dave would be a general partner, and Kevin would be a limited partner.

(2) Liability. Would Dave's liability be different from Kevin's?

Yes. In order to take an active role in running the business, Dave would have to be a general partner and accept unlimited liability. Since Kevin will invest money and share in the profits, but will not manage the business, he could be a limited partner and will have limited liability.

(3) Return on Investment. Explain how the expected return on equity of this business would be affected if the business could achieve the same net income in the first year with only $40,000 of equity instead of $60,000.

The business would achieve a higher return on equity if it could rely on a smaller amount of equity. In the first year, its ROE would be 25% if it uses $40,000 in equity, versus 17% if it uses $60,000 in equity.

(4) Business Risk. Describe the risk of this business.

The risk is that the firm either experiences higher expenses or lower revenue than anticipated. Thus, its earnings could be less than anticipated. The firm could even fail if the revenue is much lower than expenses, which could cause the owners to lose all of their investment.

Web Insight — Franchising at Domino's Pizza

At the opening of the chapter, Domino's Pizza was introduced. Go to the website (www.franchise.org/Dominos_Pizza_franchise.aspx) or select another related website by using the search terms "Domino's" and "franchising." Summarize the comments made about qualifications and training for a Domino's Pizza franchise.

Domino's wants people to have business experience before they start a franchise.

Dell's Secret for Success

Go to Dell's website (www.dell.com) and click on the link "About Dell," near the bottom of the web page. Review the section called "Investors." You can also review a recent annual report of Dell for more information.

(1) Form of Ownership. Could Dell have achieved its existing level of business if it had been organized as a partnership instead of a corporation? Explain.

> Dell has become a very large company, which is obvious from reading the annual report. It would not be able to raise the funds that it needs if it was a partnership. As a corporation, it has much better access to funding to finance its growth.

(2) Change in Form of Ownership. When Michael Dell created the company in 1984, do you think Dell was a corporation?

> Dell would not need to be a corporation until it had grown and proved that it may be a good investment for shareholders.

(3) Advantage of a Corporation. What do you think caused Dell to become a corporation?

> It needed access to investor funds in order to expand.

Video Exercise — Lessons in Forms of Business Ownership

Many free business videos are available on websites such as YouTube (www.youtube.com), and more are added every day. Search for a recent video clip about an existing business that offers lessons on "business ownership" in YouTube or any other website that provides video clips.

(1) Main Lesson. What is the name of the business in the video clip? Is the video clip focused on a proprietorship, a partnership, or a corporation? What is the main lesson of the video clip that you watched?

> Answers will vary among students. The main point is to ensure that students take the initiative to access and watch a related video and recognize the main lesson provided by the video.

(2) Shift in Business Ownership. Some related video clips explain the evolution of a business from proprietor to partnership to corporation. What do you think is the main reason for the shift in business ownership?

> Growth in the business requires other resources (perhaps technology, buildings, machinery, or employees), which requires funding.

(3) Adjustment for the Entrepreneur. Some related videos illustrate how the shift to the corporate form of ownership is a difficult adjustment for the entrepreneur. Why? How does the business decision-making process change in a manner that affects the entrepreneur?

When an entrepreneur decides to convert the business to a corporation, other investors who provide equity funding gain partial ownership. The entrepreneur loses some control as ownership is spread among other owners.

Chapter 6: Entrepreneurship and Business Planning

Introduction

The **Learning Objectives** for this chapter are to:

1. Identify the advantages and disadvantages of being an entrepreneur and creating a business.

2. Identify the market conditions that should be assessed before entering a market.

3. Explain how a new business can develop a competitive advantage.

4. Explain how to develop a business plan.

5. Identify the risks to which a business is exposed, and explain how they can be managed.

1. Creating a New Business

Offer examples of various businesses created by one or a few people that were successful.

1.1 Advantages of Being an Entrepreneur

- You may earn large profits from your business and therefore have a higher income than if you worked for another business.
- You can be your own boss.
- You are in control and don't have to fear being mistreated or fired.
- You are directly rewarded for your work.

1.2 Disadvantages of Being an Entrepreneur

- You may possibly incur large losses.
- You are responsible for the business.
- You could lose your source of income if the business fails.

1.3 Entrepreneurial Profile

- Risk tolerance
- Creativity
- Initiative

2. Assessing Market Conditions

Before creating a new business for a particular market, the following conditions in that market should be considered:

2.1 Demand

There must be a strong demand for the products to be produced by the new business. Demand for any product changes over time in response to economic conditions and consumer tastes and preferences.

2.2 Competition

If the market has less competition, it is easier to enter.

2.3 Labor Conditions

Labor costs are very high in some industries. Consider the labor environment in order to estimate the labor costs of producing the products.

2.4 Regulatory Conditions

Some industries are much more heavily regulated than others.

2.5 Summary of Market Conditions

3. Developing a Competitive Advantage

Once a firm has identified and assessed its major competitors, it must develop a strategy to enable it to compete successfully against them.

3.1 Common Strategies

- Produce products efficiently — if a firm produces products efficiently, it maintains relatively low expenses and can charge a lower price.
- Produce higher-quality products — if a firm can produce a better quality product without incurring excessive costs, it has a competitive advantage over other firms in the same price range.

3.2 Using the Internet to Create a Competitive Advantage

- A web-based business may increase revenue because it may be able to replace a store; it can reduce expenses, especially when it provides services in the form of information; and it can reach additional customers.

3.3 Expenses of a Web-Based Business

- Expenses of a web-based business include the costs of developing a website, installing a shopping cart system on the site to accept orders, screening credit card payments, paying website firms to host the site, and increasing visibility to customers.

3.4 Using SWOT Analysis to Develop a Competitive Advantage

Analyze strengths, weaknesses, opportunities, and threats

4. Developing the Business Plan

A **business plan** is a detailed description of the proposed business. The business plan is not just for the entrepreneur, but also for potential **creditors** and **investors** who may consider financing the business.

4.1 Assessment of the Business Environment

- Economic environment — is assessed to determine the demand for the new product
- Industry environment — is assessed to determine the degree of competition
- Global environment — is assessed to determine how the demand for a product may be influenced by factors such as foreign country conditions and competition from foreign firms, changes in exchange rates, and changes in trade regulations

4.2 Management Plan

- Organizational structure — identifies the roles and responsibilities of the employees hired by the firm. This part of the plan should include a job description for each employee. The plan should indicate how the structure would change as the firm grows.
- Production — describes the production process, such as the location of production facilities and the design and layout of the facilities
- Human resources — explains how employees will be motivated, managed, and compensated to ensure that they will perform well for the firm

4.3 Marketing Plan

- Target market — identifies the profile of customers who would purchase the products
- Product characteristics — will differentiate the new firm's product from those of competitors
- Pricing strategy — considers prices of competing products and the cost per unit of producing the product
- Distribution strategy — identifies how the product will be distributed to customers (through retailers versus wholesalers versus directly to consumers)
- Promotion strategy — should consider the target market and pricing strategy

4.4 Financial Plan

- Financing strategy — the amount of financing necessary and the proportion obtained from other owners versus investors
- Feasibility of business — estimation of benefits versus costs of the business. Revenue should be forecasted based on expected sales volume and product price. Estimated expenses are based on the plans for organizational structure, location, design, and plant layout, along with the production volume. This analysis is important to creditors and owners who will only provide funding if they believe that the business will be successful.

4.5 Online Resources for Developing a Business Plan

4.6 Summary of a Business Plan

4.7 Assessing a Business Plan

5. Risk Management by Entrepreneurs

5.1 Reliance on One Customer
The customer's decision to buy from a competitor would cause a major loss in sales.

5.2 Reliance on One Supplier
The business may be severely affected if that supplier does not fulfill its obligations.

5.3 Reliance on a Key Employee
The death or resignation of the employee could have a severe impact on the firm's performance.

5.4 Exposure to E-risk
Electronic data could be stolen.

Solutions to End-of-Chapter Exercises

Concept Review Questions

(1) Business Planning and Value. Why does a firm's business plan affect its performance and value?

The business plan determines how the firm will use management, marketing, and financing strategies. A better plan will result in higher revenue, lower expenses, and therefore a higher value.

(2) Entrepreneur Advantages. What are the advantages of being an entrepreneur?

The advantages of being an entrepreneur are that:
- You may earn large profits on your business and therefore have a higher income than if you worked for another business.
- You can be your own boss.
- You are in control and don't have to fear being mistreated or fired.
- You are directly rewarded for your work.

(3) Entrepreneur Disadvantages. What are disadvantages of being an entrepreneur?

The disadvantages of being an entrepreneur are:
- You may possibly incur large losses.
- You are responsible for the business.
- You could lose your source of income if the business fails.

(4) Assessing Market Conditions. Suppose that you have an idea for a new business. Identify the market conditions that you would assess to determine whether to create the business.

- **Demand** — there must be a strong demand for the products to be produced by the new business. Demand for any product changes over time in response to economic conditions, consumer tastes and preferences.

- **Competition** — if the market has less competition, it is easier to enter.

- **Labor Conditions** — labor costs are very high in some industries. Consider the labor environment in order to estimate the labor costs of producing the products.

- **Regulatory Conditions** — some industries are much more heavily regulated than others.

(5) Competitive Advantage. Explain how a firm's production and pricing decisions could help it achieve a competitive advantage.

- **Prepare products efficiently** — if firm produces products efficiently, it maintains relatively low expenses and can charge a lower price.

- **Produce higher quality products** — if a firm can produce a better quality product without incurring excessive costs, it has a competitive advantage over other firms in the same price range.

(6) Categories of a Business Plan. Explain the four key parts of a business plan, and briefly describe each part.

All of the following are included in a business plan:
a. **Business environment** — economic, industry, and global environment
b. **Management plan** — organizational structure, production, and human resources
c. **Marketing plan** — target market, product characteristics, pricing, distribution, and promotion
d. **Financial plan** — amount of financing, type of financing, and feasibility of the proposed business

(7) Management Plan. The management plan is a component of the business plan. What does it contain?

- **Organizational structure** — identifies the roles and responsibilities of the employees hired by the firm. This part of the plan should include a job description for each employee. The plan should indicate how the structure would change as the firm grows.

- **Production** — describes the production process, such as the location of production facilities and the design and layout of the facilities

- **Human resources** — explains how employees will be motivated, managed, and compensated to ensure that they will perform well for the firm

(8) Marketing Plan. The marketing plan is a component of the business plan. What does it contain?

- **Target market** — identifies the profile of customers that would purchase the products

- **Product characteristics** — will differentiate the new firm's product from those of competitors

- **Pricing strategy** — considers prices of competing products and the cost per unit of producing the product

- **Distribution strategy** — identifies how the product will be distributed to customers (through retailers versus wholesalers versus directly to consumers)

- **Promotion strategy** — should consider the target market and pricing strategy

(9) Revised Business Plan. A business plan is periodically revised even after the firm is created and evolves. Why do you think a business plan is revised?

A business plan will change over time as the business evolves and market conditions change. As a firm attempts to obtain loans over time, creditors will provide loans only if they understand the firm's plans and believe that the plans are feasible.

(10) Business Plan. What are some common characteristics of a business that could make it very risky?

- Reliance on one customer — business performance will decline substantially if the customer switches to a competitor

- Reliance on one supplier — the business may be severely affected if that supplier does not fulfill its obligations

- Reliance on a key employee — death or resignation of that employee could have a severe impact on the firm's performance

- Exposure to e-risk — electronic data could be stolen

Class Communication Questions

(1) Profile of an Entrepreneur. Are people born entrepreneurs, or can they develop the skills to become an entrepreneur?

Some students may argue that you are born with entrepreneurial skills. However, people who make the effort to monitor various markets commonly recognize possible business ideas that could satisfy customers, are not subject to excessive competition, and could be profitable if managed properly.

(2) Purchasing a Business. Weigh the tradeoffs of starting a new business versus purchasing a very successful business that is currently for sale. Why might you decide to start your own business instead of purchasing a successful business?

A high price must be paid for a very successful business. You may not be able to afford to purchase a successful business. You can start your own business with less money.

(3) Why Businesses Fail. Entrepreneurs must recognize the key factors that make a business risky so that they can reduce their exposure to the risk. What do you think is the key reason why some businesses fail? (Is it because the business idea is weak, or because of bad management decisions, bad marketing decisions, or bad finance decisions?)

Answers will vary, but the primary goal is to ensure that students consider what is involved in management decisions, marketing decisions, and finance decisions.

Small Business Case — Creating a Business

Alys Navarro used to tutor her friends in math for free. She realized that she was very effective at tutoring and has decided to create a math tutoring business. She will not just try to explain the concepts, but will create a set of questions that can help students determine whether they really understand the concepts. She views this strategy as a competitive advantage over other students who already provide math tutorial services. Alys established this business with very little funding because she does not need an office to provide the service. She will rely on cheap advertising in the school newspaper and will post messages on bulletin boards for students who may need to hire a tutor. She also hopes to receive referrals from previous customers.

(1) Impact of Competition on Demand. Why might the demand for the math tutorial services offered by Alys change over time in response to the competition?

If new competitor tutorial services (such as new students who offer tutoring) enter the market, an existing firm will likely lose some of its business.

(2) Establishing a Competitive Advantage. How do you think customers who rely on Alys for the tutorial service will judge whether her service was worthwhile?

The customers may judge the work based on how they perform on exams in the course. Thus, if the tutorial service helps the customers improve by giving practice exams, this may be a competitive advantage.

(3) Risk of Business Expansion. If Alys expands her business by hiring new employees, why might she possibly lose her competitive advantage over time?

Some of the tutors who were hired may quit and start their own business and use the same competitive advantage in their own business.

(4) Risk of a Business Dominated by One Person. Explain why the math tutorial business is risky as a result of heavy reliance on one owner.

If Alys becomes ill or for any reason needs to reduce her time dedicated to work, the performance of her business will decline.

Web Insight — Entrepreneurship at Amazon.com

At the opening of the chapter, Amazon.com was introduced. Amazon.com is a great example of entrepreneurship, not only because of the business it created, but because it continues to rely on entrepreneurship for its expansion plans. Go to the website (www.amazon.com) and click on Investor Relations at the bottom of the website and then go to the annual reports section (or you could do a web search using "Amazon.com" and "Annual Report" as search terms). Review the Letter to Shareholders. Summarize the comments made about Amazon.com's future business opportunities.

Amazon.com has grown substantially, but it still has potential for more growth. In recent years, it has expanded its business internationally.

Dell's Secret for Success

Go to Dell's website (www.dell.com) and click on the link "About Dell," near the bottom of the web page. Review information about Dell's business of serving customers directly. You can also review a recent annual report of Dell for more information.

(1) Competitive Advantage. What is Dell's competitive advantage over its competitors?

Dell commonly avoids intermediaries and sells directly to customers. Also, Dell is known for its customer service. Dell has a great reputation based on its history and has expanded worldwide based on its reputation.

(2) Distribution Plan. Explain how Dell benefits from selling products directly to customers rather than relying on retail stores for much of its sales.

Dell can avoid the markup that would be charged by intermediaries when it sells directly to customers.

(3) Reputation Effect. Explain how Dell's reputation can create a competitive advantage.

Dell's reputation creates trust, so customers are willing to order products directly from Dell because they believe Dell will accommodate their requests. Customers may not be so comfortable ordering computers online with some companies.

Video Exercise — Lessons in Entrepreneurship

Many free business videos are available on websites such as YouTube (www.youtube.com), and more are added every day. Search for a recent video clip about an existing business that offers lessons on "entrepreneurship" in YouTube or any other website that provides video clips.

(1) Main Lesson. What is the name of the business in the video clip? Is the video clip focused on the creation of a business idea, the development of a business plan, or some other aspect of entrepreneurship? What is the main lesson of the video clip that you watched?

Answers will vary among students. The main point is to ensure that students take the initiative to access and watch a related video and recognize the main lesson provided by the video.

(2) Impact of Timing. Some video clips on entrepreneurship suggest that timing is critical. Explain how timing would affect the performance of the business in your video clip. For example, how might a change in market conditions affect this business?

A change in market conditions would affect the demand for the product, or the competition, or labor conditions, or regulations. Any of these factors could affect the revenue or expenses of the firm and therefore the performance of the firm. In general, a business would prefer to time its entrance into a market when demand for the product is high and competition is low.

(3) Competitive Advantage. Does the business in your video clip have a competitive advantage? If so, what is it? That is, what makes this business successful?

Common answers include the ability to build a better product or to produce it at a lower cost (production efficiency).

Solutions to End-of-Part Exercises (Part II)

Video on Managing a Business — Adjusting the Business Plan

The Small Business Administration plays a very important role in helping many small businesses. Its website, which offers a wide range of services and information for small businesses, has a section called Delivering Success (www.sba.gov/tools/audiovideo/

deliveringsuccess/index.html) that provides video clips of small business success stories. Go to this website, and watch the video called "Business Reality Check" (total time of clip is 8 minutes, 50 seconds).

In this video clip, the success stories of two small businesses are described. Each business had a specific business plan that was altered as a result of the business environment. One business adjusted its plans as it recognized that it could achieve more efficiency by revising its target customers. The other business (based in New Orleans) had to change its business plan when hurricane Katrina hit, and many local residents were evacuated. While the two businesses are not related, they both enjoyed success as a result of having the flexibility to adjust their business in response to abrupt changes in their business environment. While they could not fully prepare for the unexpected, they quickly responded to the events that altered their business environment.

(1) Impact of Form of Business on Business Planning. Explain how the business plan (Chapter 6) is highly dependent on the form of business ownership that is planned (Chapter 5).

The form of a business determines the range of possible funding that is available. In general, a sole proprietorship has access to very limited funding, while a partnership has access to more funding (since there are more owners involved who can invest their own funds in the business). The amount of funding available affects the amount of funds that the business can invest in facilities and machinery. Thus, the business plan regarding investment is dependent on the form of business ownership.

(2) How a Change in Form of Business Alters the Business Plan. Explain how a change in the form of business ownership (Chapter 5) affects the business plan (Chapter 6).

As the form of business ownership changes, the planned amount of spending must be adjusted. When a sole proprietorship becomes a partnership, this may increase funding, which can increase the planned amount of investment in facilities by the business. When a partnership plans to convert into a publicly traded corporation, this allows much greater access to funding, and the business plan can be adjusted to allow for much more investment by the firm in machinery and facilities.

(3) Impact of Business Planning on Form of Ownership. How might the form of business ownership (Chapter 5) be affected by the business plan (Chapter 6)?

When entrepreneurs create a business, they may decide on the form of business ownership that suits their preferences. For example, if they want to retain full ownership, they will choose a sole proprietorship. As they continually assess the business conditions, they may adjust their plan in response to conditions, and at this point, the plan could influence the form of ownership. For example, if their goal is to achieve substantial growth, they may need to become a public corporation in order to attract a large amount of funding.

Chapter 7: Managing Effectively

Introduction

The **Learning Objectives** for this chapter are to:

1. Identify the levels of management.

2. Identify the key functions of mangers.

3. Describe the skills that managers need.

4. Describe methods that managers can use to utilize their time effectively.

1. Levels of Management

1.1 Top Management — includes positions such as president, chief executive officer, chief financial officer, and vice-president. They each make decisions regarding the firm's long-run objectives.

1.2 Middle Management — includes positions such as regional manager and plant manager. Middle managers resolve short-term problems and devise methods to improve performance.

1.3 Supervisory Management — includes positions such as account manager and office manager. Supervisors are highly involved with the employees who engage in the day-to-day production process.

2. Functions of Managers

2.1 Planning — Planning prepares the firm for future business conditions.

The first step is to establish **mission statement,** which describes the firm's primary goals and the strategies that will be used to achieve the firm's mission.
- Strategic plan — is intended to identify the firm's main business focus over a long-term period, perhaps three to five years
- Tactical planning — focuses on a shorter time period, such as the next year or two. These smaller-scale plans, prepared by high-level and middle-level managers, are consistent with the firm's strategic (long-term) plans.
- Operational planning — establishes the methods used for the near future (such as the next year) to achieve the tactical plans

- Contingency planning — contains alternative plans of action developed for a variety of possible business conditions

2.2 Organizing
Organization of employees and other resources in a manner that is consistent with the firm's goals. Once a firm's goals are established (from the planning function), resources are then acquired and arranged to achieve those goals.

2.3 Leading — Management process where managers influence the habits of others to achieve a common goal
- Autocratic leadership — retains full authority for decision making
- Free-rein leadership — delegates much authority to the employees
- Participative leadership — encourages some input from employees, but uses authority to make decisions

The most appropriate leadership style may be dependent on the attitudes and abilities of employees. If employees have good abilities and want to help managers improve the operations, a free-rein leadership style may be appropriate. If they do not have any interest in the firm, an autocratic leadership style may be necessary.

2.4 Controlling — monitoring and evaluation of tasks
- Correcting deficiencies
- Correcting standards
- Control of management process
- Control of reporting

2.5 Integration of Management Functions

2.6 Use of Technology to Improve Management Functions

2.7 Software to Improve Management Functions

3. **Managerial Skills**

3.1 Conceptual Skills — enable managers to see how all the functional pieces of an organization fit together. Top and middle-level mangers need this skill.

3.2 Interpersonal Skills — Communication with customers is required to ensure customer satisfaction. Communication with employees is needed to give instructions and receive feedback from employees.

3.3 Technical Skills — enable managers to understand the tasks they manage. Managers closer to the production process will tend to use their technical skills more frequently than high-level managers.

3.4 Decision-Making Skills — enable managers to determine how the firm's resources should be allocated in order to improve the firm's value

3.5 Summary of Management Skills

4. How Managers Manage Time
Time management represents the manner by which managers allocate their time when managing tasks.

4.1 Set Proper Priorities — focus attention on the activities that will yield the greatest added value to the firm

4.2 Schedule Long Time Intervals for Large Tasks — focus attention on a single task

4.3 Minimize Interruptions

4.4 Set Short-term Goals — to achieve consistent progress on large tasks

4.5 Delegate Some Tasks to Employees

Solutions to End-of-Chapter Exercises

Concept Review Questions

(1) Strategic Planning and Value. Explain why a firm's strategic plan affects its value.

The strategic plan determines the main focus of the firm over the next three to five years, and therefore has a major impact on the products to be produced and the revenue to be generated by the firm. The strategic plan also influences the production process and therefore the expenses of the firm. Since the performance of the firm is affected by the strategic plan, the value of the firm is affected as well.

(2) Levels of Management. Explain the responsibilities of each of the three levels of management.

Top management includes positions such as president, chief executive officer, chief financial officer, and vice-president. They each make decisions regarding the firm's long-run objectives. Middle management includes positions such as regional manager and plant manager. Middle managers resolve short-term problems and devise methods to improve performance. Supervisory (first-line) management includes positions such as account manager and office manager. Supervisors are highly involved with the employees who engage in the day-to-day production process.

(3) Mission Statement. Why does a firm create a mission statement?

The first step in planning a business is to establish **mission statement,** which describes a firm's primary goals and the strategies that will be used to achieve the firm's mission.

(4) Strategic Planning. What is a strategic plan, and how is it related to the firm's mission statement?

Strategic planning is intended to identify the firm's main business focus over a long-term period, perhaps three to five years. This plan is intended to satisfy the firm's mission.

(5) Tactical Planning. What is tactical planning, and how is it related to the firm's strategic plan? What is operational planning, and how is it related to the tactical planning?

Tactical planning focuses on a shorter time period, such as the next year or two. These smaller-scale plans, prepared by high-level and middle-level managers, are consistent with the firm's strategic (long-term) plans. Operational planning establishes the methods used for the near future (such as the next year) to achieve the tactical plans.

(6) Organizing. Describe the organizing function and explain how it is used to achieve the firm's goals.

Organizing is the organization of employees and other resources in a manner that is consistent with the firm's goals. Once a firm's goals are established (from the planning function), resources are then acquired and arranged to achieve those goals.

(7) Leadership Styles. Explain the common leadership styles used by managers. Explain why the attitudes and abilities of employees may affect the most appropriate leadership style to be applied.

There are three common leadership styles:
- Autocratic leaders retain full authority for decision making.
- Free-rein leaders delegate much authority to the employees.
- Participative leaders encourage some input from employees, but use their authority to make decisions.

The most appropriate leadership style may be dependent on the attitude and abilities of employees. If employees have good abilities and want to help managers improve the operations, a free-rein leadership style may be appropriate. If they do not have any interest in the firm, an autocratic leadership style may be necessary.

(8) Managers Skills. Describe the different types of skills that managers need.

- Conceptual skills enable managers to see how all the functional pieces of an organization fit together. Top and middle-level mangers need this skill.

- Interpersonal skills include communication with customers to ensure customer satisfaction, and communication with employees to give instructions and receive feedback from employees.

- Technical skills enable managers to understand the tasks they manage. Managers closer to the production process will tend to use their technical skills more frequently than high-level managers.

- Decision-making skills enable managers to determine how the firm's resources should be allocated in order to improve the firm's value.

(9) Time Management. Explain how time management could be used to efficiently complete a long-term project.

First, set proper priorities, which means giving this project much attention. Schedule long time intervals for large tasks related to this project. Minimize interruptions. Set short-term goals so that you consistently make progress on the project. Delegate some tasks involved in this project to other employees if possible.

(10) Controlling Function. Explain why the controlling function would be important when monitoring the development of a long-term project such as building a production plant.

The controlling process is necessary to monitor the plans and ensure that there is continual progress. In addition, the controlling process can be used to evaluate each step of the project to ensure it is done correctly before moving on to the next step.

Class Communication Questions

(1) Challenge for High-Level Management. In a large corporation, high-level managers make key decisions about the type of product to produce, the location of the production plant, the size of the business (number of employees), the size and layout of the production plant, the marketing of the product, and financing. What do you think is the most challenging task for high-level management?

Answers will vary, but the primary goal is to ensure that students consider the various tasks of high-level management.

(2) Management Functions. If you were a manager of a retail store, which management function would be most important for you to be successful? Why?

Answers will vary. Organizing is important to ensure that the store is run efficiently. Leading may be necessary to ensure that employees perform well. Controlling is necessary to evaluate whether any changes in the store are necessary.

(3) Management Skills. If you were a manager of a retail store, which management skill would be necessary for you to be successful? Why?

Answers will vary. Interpersonal skills are necessary to communicate with your employees and customers in the store. Decision-making skills will have a major impact on the future performance of the business.

Small Business Case — Using Management Skills

Tom Lancer is the owner of Zycles Company, which produces and sells motorcycles. Tom requires much interaction among the managers who manage the company. The supervisory managers interact with the assembly-line workers on a daily basis. The middle managers are heavily involved with selling the motorcycles to various dealerships. They determine what types of motorcycles the dealerships want to buy, and they also respond to complaints from dealerships about previous orders. The middle managers interact with the supervisory managers when problems occur with the assembly-line production. The high-level managers determine the future design of the motorcycles, how to finance future operations, and how to advertise the company's products. They consider information provided by the middle managers before making key decisions.

(1) Impact of Feedback from Managers on Decisions. Why should high-level managers consider feedback from middle managers?

Middle managers are closer to the operations and to dealerships than high-level managers, and they will be able to provide input in response to plans by high-level managers to ensure that the plans satisfy the dealerships.

(2) Impact of Interpersonal Skills. If Zycles Company wants to create a better design for its motorcycles to improve customer satisfaction, why is it important that its managers have good interpersonal skills?

The managers need to obtain feedback from customers and to listen to customer complaints in order to recognize how the design of the company's motorcycles can be improved. The managers need to interact with customers so that they understand why dealerships and customers are not satisfied and what customers want.

(3) Impact of Conceptual Skills. The high-level managers of Zycles Company are aware that many of its customers are under 30 years of age. They want to consider how to change their image so that they can also appeal to customers who are older than 30. Why are conceptual skills needed to achieve this goal?

Conceptual skills are needed to understand how a firm's image influences the types of customers that purchase motorcycles from the firm.

(4) Time Management. Zycles Company's managers will soon provide the engineers with input and ask them to redesign some motorcycles for next year. They request that the engineers focus completely on this task over a two-week period rather than allocate an hour a day over a period of three months. What is the benefit of concentrating the effort?

The engineers will be more focused if they can allocate all their time to the new design rather than if they allow only a small portion of each day for this task.

Web Insight — Managing at LA Fitness

At the opening of the chapter, LA Fitness was introduced. Go to the website (www.lafitness .com) and review the information about the company. Based on the club's operations, what key functions are required of LA Fitness managers? What skills do its managers need?

The managers of LA Fitness need interpersonal skills to ensure that its employees are motivated to satisfy customers. The managers may also need to listen to customer input regarding preferences (specific workout facilities) that LA Fitness can provide.

Dell's Secret for Success

Go to Dell's website (www.dell.com) and click on the link "About Dell," near the bottom of the web page. You can also review a recent annual report of Dell for more information.

(1) Mission. What is Dell's mission or objectives?

Dell's mission is to be a great company in many ways. That mission statement is very broad, but it lists objectives of serving customers, employees, and shareholders.

(2) Strategic Planning. What strategic plans does Dell use to achieve its mission?

Its goals are to ensure high satisfaction of its customers, to be a great workplace for its employees, and to provide a superior return to its shareholders. Its high-quality products attract a strong demand. It focuses on keeping its expenses are low. Thus, it can charge a relatively low price for its products and still make profits.

(3) Benefits of Planning. Explain why the planning process and the organizing function of managers are critical for a growing company like Dell.

Dell's growth is dependent on planning, and this requires organizing skills. If the plans are not organized, the growth might not plan for proper production facilities to satisfy the demand for products.

Video Exercise — Lessons in Leadership

Many free business videos are available on websites such as YouTube (www.youtube.com), and more are added every day. Search for a recent video clip about an existing business that offers lessons on "leadership" in YouTube or any other website that provides video clips.

(1) Main Lesson. What is the name of the business in the video clip? Is the video clip focused on how to develop leadership skills, how to convert employees into leaders, or some other aspect of entrepreneurship? What is the main lesson of the video clip that you watched?

> Answers will vary among students. The main point is to ensure that students take the initiative to access and watch a related video and recognize the main lesson provided by the video.

(2) Leadership. In what ways can a leader improve a firm's performance? If examples are provided in the video you watched, mention them here.

> Leaders can motivate other employees so that they are willing to work harder. This could increase the sales efforts and therefore increase revenue. It could also increase efficiency and therefore reduce expenses.

(3) Leader's Environment. Some videos suggest that a leader needs the right type of business workplace environment in order to lead properly. Offer an example of a situation in which a manager with good leadership skills is ineffective because of conditions in the workplace.

> If a manager attempts to lead employees, but has no power to make employees listen, then the manager may be ineffective.

Chapter 8: Organizational Structure

Introduction

The **Learning Objectives** for this chapter are to:

1. Explain the purpose of an organizational structure and how organizational structure varies among firms.

2. Explain how accountability can be achieved in an organizational structure.

3. Describe how centralized and decentralized organizational structures differ.

4. Discuss methods firms can use to obtain employee input.

5. Identify methods that can be used to departmentalize tasks.

1. Purpose and Types of Organizational Sructure   Characteristics

1.1 Chain of Command

1.2 How Organizational Structure Varies Among Firms

- Span of control — number of employees managed by each manager. A narrow span of control is designed to have each manager supervise just a few employees. A wide span of control is designed to have each manager supervise a large number of employees.
- Organizational height — number of layers in the structure from bottom to top. A tall organization has a relatively large number of layers. A flat organization has relatively few layers.
- Line versus staff positions — line positions are established to make decisions that achieve specific business goals. Staff positions are established to support the efforts of line positions, rather than to achieve specific goals of the firm.
- A line organization is an organization that contains only line positions and no staff positions.
- An organization that has both line and staff positions and that assigns authority from higher-level managers to employees is called a **line-and-staff organization**.

1.3 Impact of Information Technology on Organizational Structure

2. Accountability in an Organizational Structure
Job descriptions can ensure accountability.

2.1 Role of the Board of Directors

The board is the set of executives responsible for monitoring the activities of the firm's president and other high-level managers. It approves key business proposals made by the firm's top management. In general, the board is not involved in managing the day-to-day activities of the firm.

- Inside board members — employees of the firm
- Outside board members — not employed by the firm and therefore more likely to ensure that policies are consistent with shareholders interests.
- Conflicts of interest — occur within the board because inside managers may make decisions that serve management rather than shareholders. Outside directors may sometimes be subject to conflicts of interest as well.
- Board committees:
  - Compensation committee
  - Nominating committee
  - Audit committee

2.2 Oversight of the Internal Auditor

The auditor ensures that all departments follow the firm's guidelines and procedures.

2.3 Internal Control Process

The Sarbanes-Oxley Act requires publicly traded firms to establish processes for internal controls to more accurately monitor their financial performance over time.

3. Distributing Authority Among the Job Positions

3.1 Centralization

Centralized firms maintain most authority among the high-level managers.

3.2 Decentralization

A decentralized firm spreads authority among many groups and levels of managers. An extreme form of decentralization is autonomy, in which divisions make their own decisions and act independently.

- Advantages
  - Reduces operating expenses, as some positions are eliminated
  - Shortens the decision-making process, since managers at lower levels can make decisions
  - Improves morale of employees at lower levels as they have more responsibilities.
- Disadvantages
  - Requires decisions by lower-level managers who may lack experience to make proper decisions
  - Middle and supervisory managers may be overwhelmed with additional responsibilities
- The proper degree of decentralization depends on the skills of the managers who could be assigned additional responsibilities.

4. Structures That Allow More Employee Input

4.1 Matrix organization — employees from various parts of the firm focus on a specific project. Employeees can contribute different perspectives toward solving problems. But none of the employees may feel responsible for ensuring that goals are met.

4.2 Intrapreneurship — process of encouraging specific employees within an organization to create ideas, as if they were entrepreneurs who were running their own businesses.

4.3 Informal Organizational Structure — informal communications network among a firm's employees, called the grapevine. It allows more interaction and friendships among employees, but can sometimes be used to spread incorrect or negative information about the firm.

5. Methods of Departmentalizing Tasks

5.1 Departmentalize by Function — organizes tasks and responsibilities according to employee functions

5.2 Departmentalize by Product — organizes tasks and responsibilities according to the type of product being produced. Many large firms departmentalize by both product and function.

5.3 Departmentalize by Location — organizes the business by geographic regions

5.4 Departmentalize by Customer — organizes the company into departments based on the type of customer.

Solutions to End-of-Chapter Exercises

Concept Review Questions

(1) Organizational Structure. How can a firm's organizational structure affect its value?

An organizational structure is a structure within the firm that identifies job responsibilities for each job position and the relationships among those positions. Decisions about the organizational structure affect the efficiency with which a firm produces its product, which affects the firm's expenses and therefore its value.

(2) Span of Control. Explain how the span of control can vary among firms.

The span of control represents the number of employees managed by each manager. A narrow span of control is designed to have each manager supervise just a few employees. A wide span of control is designed to have each manager supervise a large number of employees.

(3) Organizational Height. Explain how the organizational height can vary among firms.

The Organizational height represents the number of layers in the structure of a firm from bottom to top. A tall organization has a relatively large number of layers, while a flat organization has relatively few layers.

(4) Line Versus Staff. Compare the role of line positions versus staff positions. Compare the structure of line organizations versus line-and-staff organizations.

Line positions are established to make decisions that achieve specific business goals. **Staff positions** are established to support the efforts of line positions, rather than to achieve specific goals of the firm. A **line organization** is an organization that contains only line positions and no staff positions. An organization that has both line and staff positions and that assigns authority from higher-level managers to employees is called a **line-and-staff organization**.

(5) Board Composition. Compare inside board members versus outside board members. Explain why conflicts can occur between them.

The **board of directors** is a set of executives responsible for monitoring the activities of the firm's president and other high-level managers. It approves key business proposals made by the firm's top management. In general, the board is not involved in managing the day-to-day activities of the firm. **Inside board members** are employees of the firm. **Outside board members** are not employed by the firm and therefore are more likely to ensure that policies are consistent with shareholders' interests. **Conflicts of interest** within the board occur because inside managers may make decisions that serve management rather than shareholders. Outside directors may sometimes be subject to conflicts of interest as well.

(6) Board Committees. Describe the three main committees of the board of directors.

The compensation committee sets executive compensation. The nominating committee determines who will be the candidates for new board positions. The audit committee monitors the auditing of financial statements.

(7) Sarbanes-Oxley Act. Explain how the Sarbanes-Oxley Act affected the internal control process of firms.

The Sarbanes-Oxley Act requires that publicly traded firms establish a process for internal controls so that they can more effectively monitor their financial performance. This is important, because it makes the managers more accountable for monitoring the firm and ensuring that the financial information they report to shareholders is accurate.

(8) Decentralization. Compare centralization with decentralization. Explain the advantages and disadvantages of decentralization.

Centralization maintains most authority among the high-level managers, while decentralization spreads authority among many groups and levels of managers. An extreme form of decentralization is autonomy, in which divisions make their own decisions and act independently.

Advantages of decentralization are:
- Reduces the operating expenses, as some positions are eliminated
- Shortens the decision-making process, since managers at lower levels can make decisions
- Improves morale of employees at lower levels as they have more responsibilities

Disadvantages of decentralization are:
- Requires decisions by lower-level managers who may lack the experience to make proper decisions
- Middle and supervisory managers may be overwhelmed with additional responsibilities

The proper degree of decentralization depends on the skills of the managers who could be assigned additional responsibilities.

(9) Informal Structures. Explain the various informal structures that allow more employee input.

A matrix organization allows employees from various parts of the firm to focus on a specific project. Employees can contribute different perspectives toward solving problems, but none of the employees may feel responsible for ensuring that goals are met. **Intrapreneurship** is the process of encouraging specific employees within an organization to create ideas, as if they were entrepreneurs who were running their own businesses. An **informal organizational structure** is an informal communications network among a firm's employees, called the **grapevine**. It allows more interaction and friendships among employees but can sometimes be used to spread incorrect or negative information about the firm.

(10) Departmentalizing. Explain the methods of departmentalizing.

A firm can departmentalize in the following ways:
- Departmentalize by function — organizes tasks and responsibilities according to employee functions
- Departmentalize by product — organizes tasks and responsibilities according to the type of product being produced. Many large firms departmentalize by both product and function.
- Departmentalize by location — organizes the business by geographic regions
- Departmentalize by customer — organizes the company into departments based on the type of customer

Class Communication Questions

(1) Span of Control Dilemma. For a chain of clothing stores spread across the United States, do you think a narrow or a wide span of control is optimal for each store manager?

A wide span of control is optimal because a narrow span of control would require too many layers of employees.

(2) Outside Directors. Do you think outside directors are more important for a small business in which the key managers are also the owners, or a large business that has thousands of shareholders?

An outside director is important to ensure that managers make proper decisions. For a small business in which managers are also the owners, they are likely to make decisions that serve the owners. However, for a large business in which managers do not have much ownership, they may be tempted to make decisions for themselves. Inside directors may also have motives to serve themselves since they are managers. Outside directors are not managers and therefore are more likely to ensure that the managers serve the shareholders.

(3) Sarbanes-Oxley Act. The Sarbanes-Oxley Act requires that publicly traded firms establish more internal controls. Do you think that these controls are beneficial, or is this regulation causing businesses to waste money without any improvement?

Answers will vary. One argument is that a business implements internal controls only to satisfy Sarbanes-Oxley (SOX). Some businesses would argue that they already had sufficient internal controls even before SOX, but now they must waste money to create a special set of controls that do not improve the performance. However, the regulation may ensure that all publicly traded firms have some minimum level of internal controls, and this can make A firm's operations more transparent to its shareholders. That is, the controls may help to detect financial fraud so that situations such as the Enron fraud can be avoided in the future.

Small Business Case — Organizational Structure Decisions

Mars Technology Company owns small production plants in four different cities that produce high-technology products such as digital cameras and miniature computers. The firm has four divisions, each of which includes a production plant served by its supervisors, who report to top-line managers. Every division has three vice-presidents—one for finance, marketing, and production.

(1) Deciding a Span of Control. At all levels above the supervisor, the organizational structure has a narrow span of control. What is a disadvantage of this structure?

The disadvantage is that it is expensive to have many job positions that oversee only a few other positions. There is a high cost for excessive oversight.

(2) Impact on Efficiency. How might the Mars Technology Company revise its organizational structure to increase its efficiency?

> Each division might not need three vice-presidents. Perhaps the structure could be revised so that there is a vice-president for finance, marketing, and production within the entire company.

(3) Centralization Versus Decentralization. Do you think factory workers at Mars Technology Company would be more satisfied if day-to-day production decisions were centralized or if they were made at each production plant? Why?

> Decisions may be more appropriate if they are made at each production plant, because the managers at the plant are closer to the production and should be better able to make the decisions. There would still need to be general oversight of each plant.

(4) Departmentalization Decision. Mars Technology Company wants to departmentalize by product, but its divisions are in four different cities scattered across the United States. Why would it be costly for this firm to departmentalize by product in this firm?

> Each product would need to have managers, but the managers for a given product could not always be at each division and would have to travel across divisions to oversee operations related to the product to which they are assigned. It might be more efficient to department-alize by location so that managers could oversee all operations within a specific location. This would require that managers have the background to oversee the various products.

Web Insight — Operational Structure at Schwinn

At the opening of the chapter, Schwinn was introduced. Go to the website (www.schwinn.com) and review the products that Schwinn produces. Do you think that Schwinn should departmentalize tasks by product (have separate departments for bicycles, fitness equipment, and motor scooters)? Or should it departmentalize tasks by function (a marketing department would do the marketing for all products, a finance department would do the finance for all products, etc.)? Explain your answer.

> The main point is that students understand the difference. If Schwinn departmentalizes by product, it would need a separate marketing department for each product, a separate finance department for each product, etc. It would only need one marketing department and one finance department if it departmentalizes by function.

Dell's Secret for Success

Go to Dell's website (www.dell.com) and click on the link "About Dell," near the bottom of the web page. You can also review a recent annual report to obtain more information.

(1) Functions of Executives. Review Dell's organizational structure based on the position titles of its executives. What types of functions do these executives perform ?

Strategy, marketing, finance and other functions.

(2) Role of the Board. What is the role of Dell's board of directors?

Dell's board oversees the firm's main decisions, and makes sure that decisions are in the best interests of shareholders.

(3) Role of Executives. What is the general role of Dell's top-level management?

Dell's top-level management focuses on major decisions on how Dell can achieve its strategic plan.

Video Exercise — Lessons in Organizing an Effective Board of Directors

Many free business videos are available on websites such as YouTube (www.youtube.com), and more are added every day. Search for a recent video clip about an existing business that offers lessons on "board of directors" in YouTube or any other website that provides video clips.

(1) Main Lesson. What is the name of the business in the video clip? Is the video clip focused on the creation of a board of directors, or an example of problems due to a particular board structure, or some other aspect of entrepreneurship? What is the main lesson of the video clip that you watched?

Answers will vary among students. The main point is to ensure that students take the initiative to access and watch a related video and recognize the main lesson provided by the video.

(2) Board Feedback. Some videos stress that an entrepreneur who creates a board must ensure that the board is independent and willing to offer feedback. Why do you think some small businesses receive very little insight from the board?

In some cases, the board members are not qualified and do not have the ability to offer useful insight. In other cases, board members may believe that their suggestions will be ignored by managers, so they do not offer suggestions.

(3) Entrepreneur-Board Conflict. Why might some entrepreneurs prefer a board with members who do not offer much input?

Some entrepreneurs have specific goals and plans in mind for their business, and they may fear that board members will offer suggestions that conflict with these goals and plans. The ideal situation would be for the entrepreneur and board members to be in general agreement on the goals of the firm, and if the board members are capable, they should be offer some suggestions that are beneficial to the entrepreneur and the business.

Chapter 9: Improving Productivity and Quality

Introduction

The **Learning Objectives** for this chapter are to:

1. Identify the key resources used for production.

2. Identify the factors that affect the plant site decision.

3. Describe how various factors affect the design and layout decision.

4. Describe the key tasks that are involved in production control.

5. Describe the key factors that affect production efficiency.

1. Resources Used for the Production Process

A **production process** (also called conversion process) is the series of tasks in which resources are used to produce a product or service. **Production management** (also called **operations management**) attempts to develop an efficient production process by determining the proper amounts of materials to use, the proper mix of resources to use, the proper assignments of tasks, and the proper sequence of the tasks that must be performed. Effective production management can enhance the profitability and value of the firm.

1.1 Human Resources
Human resources are needed for production. The operating expenses involved in hiring human resources depend on both the number of workers and their skill level.

1.2 Materials
Materials used in the production process are normally transformed by the firm's human resources into the final product.

1.3 Other Resources
Other Resources used in production include factories, warehouses, and machinery and equipment.

1.4 Combining Resources for Production
Managers attempt to utilize resources in a manner that achieves production at low cost. Two ways of combining resources to carry out production are work stations and assembly lines.

- **Work station** — area to which one or more workers are assigned to perform a specific task. A work station can include the machinery and equipment the employees need to perform their tasks.
- **Assembly line** — consists of a sequence of work stations in which each station is designed to carry out specific phases of the production process.

2. Selecting a Site

2.1 Factors Affecting the Site Decision
- Cost of workplace space — the cost of purchasing or leasing buildings or office space can vary significantly among locations (higher in the North)
- Cost of Labor — the cost of human resources varies among locations (higher in the North, and in urban areas)
- Tax Incentives — some local governments offer tax credits and other incentives to attract businesses
- Source of Demand — service firms commonly locate close to their customers in order to reduce the cost of transporting the product and provide greater convenience to customers
- Access to Transportation — firms that sell their products across the nation need access to transportation facilities
- Supply of Labor — some firms need workers with highly specialized skills and are likely to locate in areas where they can hire the type of labor they need

2.2 Evaluating Possible Sites.
A firm must identify the criteria that affect its site decision and assign a weight to each factor reflecting its relative importance. The firm can develop a site evaluation matrix in which it assigns ratings to the criteria and then apply a weighted average of all of the ratings.

3. Selecting the Design and Layout
Once a site has been chosen, the firm must determine the design and layout of its facility.
- Design — size and structure of the facility
- Layout — arrangement of machinery and equipment within the facility

3.1 Factors Affecting Design and Layout
- Site characteristics — if land cost is high, a high-rise facility may be selected, while if land is cheap, the firm may design a facility that is all on one level.
- Production process:
  o A **product layout** (assembly-line processes) arranges task in a sequence, so all tasks should be in the same general area.
  o A **fixed-position layout** is used if the product is very large and is in one fixed position during production. The employees go to the product (ships, airplanes, homes).

- o **Flexible manufacturing** enables the firm to restructure its layout to accommodate future revisions.
- Product line — firms with narrow product lines can design more specialized facilities. Firms that produce a wider range of products must have a more flexible layout that can be changed easily when production needs change.
- Desired Production Capacity — firms must plan for growth. Facilities are often designed to make it easy for firms to increase capacity over time.

4. Production Control

4.1 Purchasing Materials
- Selecting a supplier of materials — managers evaluate such factors as the price, quality, speed, reliability, servicing, and credit availability.
- Managers may negotiate **volume discounts** when they order large quantities of materials.
- Delegating production to suppliers — managers may consider **outsourcing**, which is the act of purchasing component parts from suppliers rather than producing the components internally. They may consider **deintegration**, which is the strategy of delegating some parts of the production process if the suppliers can perform the tasks at lower cost.

4.2 Inventory Control
Inventory control is the process of managing inventory at a level that minimizes costs.
- Control of materials inventories:
  - o Carrying costs — cost of maintaining inventories
  - o Ordering costs — cost of placing orders for additional inventory as needed
  - o Tradeoff — more frequent ordering reduces carrying costs but increases ordering costs
- Control of work-in-process inventories (inventories of partially completed products) — managers control costs while avoiding shortages
- Control of inventories of finished goods — if inventories of one product increase, the firm can shift production to focus on other products, or it can pursue strategies to increase the demand for the product

4.3 Routing — sequence of tasks necessary to complete the production of a product

4.4 Scheduling — setting time periods for the completion of tasks
- Impact of technology — firms allow customers to place orders over the Internet. Orders placed at the firm's website can be filled more quickly.
- Scheduling for special projects:
  - o A **Gantt chart** shows the expected timing of each activity that must be performed to complete a project.
  - o The **program evaluation and review technique (PERT)** enables managers to schedule tasks so as to minimize delays. PERT identifies the **critical path**, which

is the sequence of tasks that takes the longest to complete. The tasks on the critical path must be completed on time to avoid delays.

4.5 Quality Control

Quality control determines whether the product meets a desired standard of quality and identifies necessary improvements. Firms may assess quality through:

- Control by technology — screens out defective parts and determines if component parts meet quality standards
- Control by employees — employees assess quality and offer suggestions for improvement using a quality control circle
- Control by sampling — randomly selects products and tests to determine if they meet the firm's quality standards
- Control by complaint monitoring — considers customer feedback on products after they have been produced, sold, and used by customers
- Correcting deficiencies — improves the production process and quality

5. Methods to Improve Production Efficiency

5.1 Technology

Technology can improve production processes. **Automation** completes work without the use of human employees.

5.2 Economies of Scale

Economies of scale reflect lower average costs as more units of product are produced.

5.3 Restructuring

Restructuring involves the revision of the production process to improve efficiency. An example is reducing the number of employees or **downsizing** to reduce costs.

5.4 Integration of the Production Tasks

Each task can be accomplished only after other tasks have been completed. The **supply chain** is the process from the beginning of the production process until the product reaches the customer.

Solutions to End-of-Chapter Exercises

Concept Review Questions

(1) Impact of Production Process on Value. Explain why management of the production process can have a major impact on the valuation of a business.

The production decisions determine the amount of funds invested in the facilities used to produce products and the production process that is used. The cost of a firm's production is dependent on these decisions. If the firm can create an efficient production process, it can maintain low expenses and achieve higher profits and higher performance. It will enhance the value of its business.

(2) Resources. Describe the resources used in the production process.

Human resources are needed for production. The operating expenses involved in hiring human resources depend on both the number of workers and their skill level. **Materials** used in the production process are normally transformed by the firm's human resources into the final product. **Other resources** used in production include factories, warehouses, and machinery and equipment. Managers attempt to utilize resources in a manner that achieves production at low cost.

(3) Combining Resources. Explain the use of work stations and assembly lines for combining resources.

A **work station** is an area to which one or more workers are assigned to perform a specific task. A work station can include the machinery and equipment the employees need to perform their tasks. An **assembly line** consists of a sequence of work stations in which each station is designed to carry out specific phases of the production process.

(4) Site Location. Explain the factors that should be considered in the site location decision.

The site location decision is influenced by the following factors:
- **Cost of workplace space** — the cost of purchasing or leasing buildings or office space can vary significantly among locations (higher in the North).
- **Cost of labor** — the cost of human resources varies among locations (higher in the North and in urban areas).
- **Tax incentives** — some local governments offer tax credits and other incentives to attract businesses.
- **Source of demand** — service firms commonly locate close to their customers in order to reduce the cost of transporting the product and provide greater convenience to customers.
- **Access to transportation** — firms that sell their products across the nation need access to transportation facilities.
- **Supply of labor** — some firms need workers with highly specialized skills and are likely to locate in areas where they can hire the type of labor they need.

(5) Production Layout. Explain the common forms of layout in the production process.

The **product layout** (assembly-line processes) tasks are arranged in the sequence that they are performed. A **fixed-position layout** product is very large and is in one fixed position during production. The employees go to the product (ships, airplanes, homes). **Flexible manufacturing** enables the firm to restructure its layout to accommodate future revisions.

(6) Delegating Production. Explain how some firms may delegate a portion of the production process to suppliers.

Managers may consider **outsourcing**, which is the act of purchasing component parts from suppliers rather than producing the components internally. They may consider **deintegration**, which is the strategy of delegating some parts of the production process if the suppliers can perform the tasks at lower cost.

(7) Materials Management. Explain the tradeoff involved when managing the inventory of materials.

Inventory control is the process of managing inventory at a level that minimizes costs. The managers want to minimize **carrying cost,** or the cost of maintaining materials inventories. They also want to minimize the **ordering cost,** or the cost of placing orders for additional inventory as needed. However, more frequent ordering reduces carrying costs but increases ordering costs.

(8) PERT. Explain the role of the program evaluation and review technique (PERT) in the production process.

The **program evaluation and review technique (PERT)** enables managers to schedule tasks so as to minimize delays. PERT identifies the **critical path**, which is the sequence of tasks that takes the longest to complete. The tasks on the critical path must be completed on time to avoid delays.

(9) Quality Control. Explain common methods used by managers to assess quality control.

- **Technology** — screens out defective parts and determines if component parts meet quality standards.

- **Employees** — assess the quality and offer suggestions for improvement using a **quality control circle**

- **Sampling** — randomly selects products and tests to determine if they meet the firm's quality standards

- **Complaint monitoring** — considers customer feedback on products after they have been produced, sold, and used by customers

(10) Production Efficiency. Explain the common methods to improve production efficiency.

- **Technology** can improve production processes. **Automation** completes work without the use of human employees.

- **Economies of scale** reflect lower average costs as more units of product are produced.

- **Restructuring** involves the revision of the production process to improve efficiency. An example is reducing the number of employees or **downsizing** to reduce costs.

Class Communication Questions

(1) Managing Machinery Versus People. Do you think it is more difficult to manage an assembly line that relies heavily on machinery or on human resources?

The management of machinery requires some technical skills. However, the management of many human resources can be challenging because it can be difficult to motivate employees and to ensure that they perform well.

(2) Tax Incentives for a Production Plant. Would your city benefit from providing more tax incentives to attract new production plants? Or do you think these new tax incentives would be unfair to the existing businesses that are not able to benefit from the new incentives? (Assume that your city cannot afford to offer tax incentives to all existing businesses.)

One argument is that tax incentives could attract more businesses, and that could improve the employment situation. However, those people who do not benefit from the tax incentives may feel that it is a waste of money, or that they are subsidizing these incentives when they pay their taxes.

(3) Quality Control Issue. Is quality control more important for a business that produces products or services?

This question is intended to emphasize that services require quality control. Most students think quality control only applies to products. Yet doctors, attorneys, accountants, and various types of instructors who provide services rely on their reputation for new business, and that reputation is based on the satisfaction of previous customers.

Small Business Case — Production Decisions

Cell One Company must decide on the proper combination of resources to use for its production of its cell phones. When it developed its business, it initially used human resources for most of its production process. Now it relies more heavily on machinery for various phases of the production process in order to reduce its operating expenses. Advances in technology now allow some components to be produced more efficiently by machines than by human resources. The human resources who were previously assigned to those production tasks have been reassigned to other jobs.

(1) Impact of Technology. Some employees believe that Cell One Company should not use technology because then it could hire more employees to perform the tasks and this would improve employee morale and provide more jobs for unemployed people. Do you agree?

A disadvantage of hiring more people is that it would be less efficient and the firm may fail if it cannot produce its product at a low cost. By trying to create more jobs, it may adversely affect its existing employees, its creditors, and its owners.

(2) Production Facility Decision. Cell One Company has its production facility in Los Angeles, California. Explain why the cost of production is higher in Los Angeles than in smaller towns. What is an advantage of having a production facility in a big city such as Los Angeles?

The production cost is higher because the cost of land is very expensive there and in most cities where the population is large. The advantage of a production facility in Los Angeles is access to transportation and a large supply of labor.

(3) Decision to Allow Employees to Work at Home. Cell One Company pays a very a high rent for its offices next to the production facility in Los Angeles. It wants to reduce office space and will let many of its office employees work at home. It will change the design of its offices so that any employees who need to be at the office can use whatever offices are available, and a specific office will not be designated to any employee. Is there a possible disadvantage of letting its employees work from home?

It may be more difficult to measure the productivity of employees if they are not working in the office, but the productivity of some job positions can be easily measured regardless of where an employee works.

(4) Use of Quality Control. Cell One Company pays close attention to quality control. It uses various machines to ensure that the cell phones it produces are made to fit the production specifications. Do you think this form of quality control will be ideal for detecting customer dissatisfaction?

The firm should also survey its customers to assess customer satisfaction. A cell phone may be produced in accordance with production specifications, but it may not necessarily satisfy customers because it may not have the features desired by customers.

Web Insight — Production at the MTV Network

At the opening of the chapter, the MTV network (owned by Viacom) was introduced. Go to the website (www.mtv.com) and review the types of shows that MTV produces. What do you think are the key resources that are needed by the MTV network to create a TV show? How can the MTV network properly control its production to ensure that it produces quality programming?

The key resources are the human resources and the equipment needed to create the TV shows. MTV can review its shows to ensure that they are acceptable. Since quality is partially based on customer satisfaction, MTV could allow a group of typical viewers to watch the show and assess it before it is broadcast on MTV's network.

Dell's Secret for Success

Go to Dell's website (www.dell.com) and click on the link "About Dell," near the bottom of the web page. Review information about Dell's production quality. You can also review a recent annual report of Dell for more information.

(1) Quality Goals. Describe Dell's goals regarding quality.

Dell strives to achieve high quality of its products, as quality is what separates it from some competitors. It has received numerous quality awards in the past.

(2) Quality Monitoring. How does Dell monitor quality?

It measures quality by the accuracy with which it fulfills orders, whether it delivers its products on time, its overall product quality (how the products function), and how the employees treat the customers. It can monitor its quality according to these measures.

(3) Quality Control. How does customer satisfaction relate to Dell's quality control?

If Dell achieves high quality, it can achieve a high level of customer satisfaction.

Video Exercise — Lessons in Production Quality

Many free business videos are available on websites such as YouTube (www.youtube.com), and more are added every day. Search for a recent video clip about an existing business that offers lessons on "production quality" in YouTube or any other website that provides video clips.

(1) Main Lesson. What is the name of the business in the video clip? Is the video clip focused on the use of technology for production, the quality control process, customer satisfaction, or some other aspect of production quality? What is the main lesson of the video clip that you watched?

Answers will vary among students. The main point is to ensure that students take the initiative to access and watch a related video and recognize the main lesson provided by the video.

(2) Assessing Quality. Some videos suggest that production quality begins with an understanding of customer preferences. Explain this point.

Production quality is ultimately judged by the customer. The business needs to produce a product that satisfies customers. It must produce the product in a manner that will satisfy customers.

(3) Motives for Outsourcing. Some related videos explain how outsourcing is necessary for the business to survive. Why do you think some businesses rely heavily on outsourcing?

Outsourcing may allow a firm to complete a part of the production process at a lower cost than what it could do on its own. This may allow the firm to reduce its expenses and charge a lower price to its customers.

Solutions to End-of-Part Exercises (Part III)

Video on Managing a Business — Managing for Success

The Small Business Administration plays a very important role in helping many small businesses. Its website, which offers a wide range of services and information for small businesses, has a section called Delivering Success (www.sba.gov/tools/audiovideo/ deliveringsuccess/index.html) that provides video clips of small business success stories. Go to this website, and watch the video called "Top 10 Business Tips" (total time of clip is 4 minutes, 30 seconds).

Some of the tips discussed in this video clip are related to the key management concepts covered in this part of the text, as discussed below:

- Businesses need to hire good employees. If entrepreneurs have good employees, they can empower their employees with various responsibilities. This allows entrepreneurs more time to focus on the most important business decisions.

- Businesses need to keep their mission in mind when making their decisions; this will allow them to make decisions that are consistent with their ultimate goals.

- Businesses need to plan for the future. Business decisions today should be made with consideration to their impact in the future.

- Businesses should have goals, and these goals should be written down so that they can be documented. The goals can be separated into short-term goals and long-term goals.

Some of the desirable characteristics of managers (described in Chapter 7) are very similar to these characteristics of a successful business. The personality of the business reflects the personality of its managers.

(1) Impact of Management Skills on the Organization Chart. Explain how effective planning, organizational, and leadership skills (Chapter 7) could affect the organization chart (Chapter 8) of a business.

If managers are organized, they may perform with few layers in the organization chart. In addition, if they lead effectively, they can give employees more responsibilities, which affects the job descriptions of employees.

(2) Impact of Planning Skills on Production Quality. Explain how effective planning skills (Chapter 7) could affect the production quality (Chapter 9) of a business.

Production quality is dependent on proper planning. If the production process was developed after careful planning, there is less likelihood of problems detected in the quality control phase.

(3) Impact of Organizational Structure on Production Quality. Explain how the organizational structure (Chapter 8) could affect the quality control process (Chapter 9).

If more job responsibilities are assigned to employees, these employees are more accountable and would likely achieve a higher level of productivity and quality. However, if they are given excessive responsibility, this could jeopardize their productivity and quality level.

Chapter 10: Motivating Employees

Introduction

The **Learning Objectives** for this chapter are to:

1. Explain how motivating employees can increase the value of a firm.

2. Describe the theories of motivation.

3. Discuss how a firm can motivate disgruntled employees.

4. Explain how a firm can improve employee motivation.

1. The Value of Motivation

If motivation can increase the work effort of employees, it could result in higher sales (increased revenue) and greater production efficiency (lower expenses), which would be reflected in better performance and a higher value for the firm.

2. Theories on Motivation

2.1 Hawthorne Studies

These studies were conducted during the late 1920s. The studies were designed to see how changes in working conditions affected worker performance. Productivity of workers increased even in response to worse conditions. The conclusion is that motivation of workers improved because they were allowed to participate and received attention.

2.2 Maslow's Hierarchy of Needs

People rank their needs into five general categories. Once they achieve their needs in one category, they are motivated to satisfy the needs of the next higher level. Firms motivate workers if they can fulfill the needs of workers. The hierarchy is as follows:

- Physiological needs — basic requirements for survival, such as food and shelter
- Safety needs — safe working conditions and job security
- Social needs — the desire to be accepted as part of a group
- Esteem needs — respect, recognition, and prestige
- Self-actualization — desire to reach one's full potential

2.3 Herzberg's Job Satisfaction Study

Some characteristics (**hygiene factors**) such as salary, working conditions, and job security must be maintained at adequate levels in order to prevent dissatisfaction. But improvements in hygiene factors do not necessarily lead to higher levels of satisfaction. Other characteristics (**motivational factors**) such as recognition, opportunities for advancement, and responsibility are necessary to increase satisfaction.

2.4 McGregor's Theory X and Theory Y
McGregor suggests two views of employees:
- Theory X — supervisors believe most workers dislike work and will avoid it whenever possible. These supervisors will exercise tight control over employees.
- Theory Y — supervisors believe employees are willing to work and accept responsibility. These supervisors will delegate authority to employees.

2.5 Theory Z
Based in part on Japanese management techniques that encourage worker participation in decision making, Theory Z attempts to improve motivation by giving workers more responsibility.

2.6 Expectancy Theory
An employee's efforts are influenced by the expected outcomes of those efforts. Therefore, employees will be motivated to achieve goals if the goals are achievable and the employees are offered a reward.

2.7 Equity Theory
An employee's compensation should be proportional to the employee's contribution to the firm.

2.8 Reinforcement Theory
Reinforcement can influence behavior.
- Positive reinforcement — provide rewards for desirable performance
- Negative reinforcement — encourage employees to behave in a way that avoids undesirable consequences

2.9 Motivational Guidelines Offered by Theories
- Compensate employees fairly to prevent job dissatisfaction.
- Assign tasks that help employees satisfy their needs (such as responsibility) and provide more job satisfaction.
- Create goals that are achievable.

3. Motivating Disgruntled Employees
A firm may not be able to motivate some of its disgruntled employees, regardless of its efforts. If disgruntled employees stay in their jobs, but avoid doing their work and continue to perform poorly, they should be disciplined and possibly fired so their bad attitudes will not affect other workers.

4. How Firms Can Improve Employee Motivation

4.1 Adequate Compensation Program
A merit system allocates pay according to performance, which is more effective than an across-the-board system. Firms may offer incentive plans to reward employees for achieving specific performance goals.
- Developing a proper compensation plan:
    - Align the compensation with business goals — ensure that workers are compensated in a manner consistent with their ability to satisfy business goals
    - Align compensation with specific employee goals — clearly specify individual employee goals
    - Set achievable goals — offer achievable bonuses (or other rewards)
    - Allow employee input — consider employees' suggestions for a plan

4.2 Job Security
Provide more job security by training employees to handle various tasks so that they can be assigned other duties if their typical assignments are no longer needed.

4.3 Flexible Work Schedule
Examples include a compressed workweek and job sharing.

4.4 Employee Involvement Programs
- Job enlargement — expands the jobs assigned to employees
- Job rotation — allows employees to periodically rotate their assignments.
- Worker empowerment — allows workers more authority
- Teamwork — allows employees with varied job positions the responsibility to achieve a specific goal
- Open-book management — the firm educates workers on their contribution to the firm and enables employees to periodically assess their own performance levels

4.5 Comparison of Methods Used to Enhance Job Satisfaction

4.6 Firms That Achieve the Highest Job Satisfaction Level

Solutions to End-of-Chapter Exercises

Concept Review Questions

(1) Impact of Motivation on Business Value. Why would an increase in the motivation of employees increase the value of the business?

If motivation can increase the work effort of employees, it could result in higher sales (increased revenue) and greater production efficiency (lower expenses), which would be reflected in better performance and a higher value for the firm.

(2) Hawthorne Studies. Explain the conclusion of the Hawthorne studies as it relates to the motivation of employees.

The studies were conducted during the late 1920s and designed to see how changes in working conditions affected worker performance. Productivity of workers increased even in response to worse conditions. The conclusion is that motivation of workers improved because they were allowed to participate and received attention.

(3) Hierarchy of Needs. Explain Maslow's hierarchy of needs theory as it relates to the motivation of employees.

According to Maslow's hierarchy of needs, people rank their needs into five general categories. Once they achieve their needs in one category, they are motivated to satisfy the needs of the next higher level. Firms motivate workers if they can fulfill the needs of workers. The hierarchy is as follows:

- **Physiological needs** — basic requirements for survival, such as food and shelter

- **Safety needs** — safe working conditions and job security

- **Social needs** — the desire to be accepted as part of a group

- **Esteem needs** — respect, recognition, and prestige

- **Self-actualization** — desire to reach one's full potential

Firms can more easily satisfy employees by understanding their prevailing hierarchy level and needs.

(4) Herzberg's Job Satisfaction. Briefly describe Herzberg's job satisfaction study on worker motivation.

Herzberg's study found that some job characteristics (**hygiene factors**) such as salary, working conditions, and job security must be maintained at adequate levels in order to prevent dissatisfaction. But improvements in hygiene factors do not necessarily lead to higher levels of satisfaction. Other job characteristics (**motivational factors**) such as recognition, opportunities for advancement, and responsibility are necessary to increase job satisfaction.

(5) Theory X and Theory Y. Compare McGregor's Theory X and Theory Y regarding supervisor perceptions of employees.

McGregor suggests two views of employees:
- **Theory X** — supervisors believe most workers dislike work and will avoid it whenever possible. These supervisors will exercise tight control over employees.
- **Theory Y** — supervisors believe employees are willing to work and accept responsibility. These supervisors will delegate authority to employees.

(6) Motivating Employees. Based on the theories of motivation provided in this chapter, offer some general conclusions about how to motivate employees.

Compensate employees fairly to prevent job dissatisfaction. Assign tasks that help employees satisfy their needs (such as responsibility) and provide more job satisfaction. Create goals that are achievable. Consider allowing employees some control over their work schedule.

(7) Employee Compensation. Explain how employee compensation can be aligned with changes in the value of a publicly traded firm. Also explain why this form of compensation is ineffective for some employees.

The firm can provide its stock to its employees as partial compensation. The compensation of employees will be higher when the firm's performance is better because the stock price will be higher under these conditions. To the extent that employees believe they can affect the value of the firm, they may be more motivated. However, if employees believe that they do not directly affect the value of the firm, they may not believe that their work effort will have any impact on their compensation.

(8) Merit System. Why does a merit system provide more motivation to employees than an across-the-board system?

A merit system rewards employees more directly for their work performance. An across-the-board system offers no reward for high performance, so there is no motivation to perform well.

(9) Employee Involvement Programs. Describe some popular employee involvement programs and explain how they may motivate employees.

Employee involvement programs include:
- Job enlargement — expands the jobs assigned to employees
- Job rotation — allows employees to periodically rotate their assignments
- Worker empowerment — allows workers more authority
- Teamwork — allows employees with varied job positions the responsibility to achieve a specific goal
- Open-book management — the firm educates workers on their contribution to the firm and enables employees to periodically assess their own performance levels

All of these programs give employees more responsibility, which may motivate them.

(10) Job Enlargement. What is a possible disadvantage of job enlargement that could reduce the morale of employees?

Employees may be overwhelmed if they are given too much responsibility and authority.

Class Communication Questions

(1) Motivation Theory in Reality. Which theory of motivation best describes the employees where you currently work or most recently worked?

In many cases, students will cite Theory X because some employees dislike work and will avoid work if possible. However, they may cite Theory Y if they know of employees who wanted more responsibility or reinforcement theory if reinforcement influences behavior.

(2) Motivation Theory from a Manager's Perspective. Which theory of motivation would you use in the environment where you currently work or most recently worked?

Students who trust that employees will do their work without being forced to may cite Theory Y or reinforcement theory or equity theory. Students who think that employees minimize their work may cite Theory X.

(3) Compensation Program in Reality. Which compensation program is used where you currently work or most recently worked? If you were the owner of the business where you work, what compensation method would you use?

Most students would likely prefer a merit system with incentive plans, so that employees are motivated to work. Many businesses still use various forms of an across-the-board system for many of their employees, which offers no motivation for employees to perform well.

Small Business Case — How Not to Motivate Employees

Players Company produces and sells sporting goods. Last year it hired eight recent college graduates for various entry-level management positions. Each person was a business major with a high grade point average and very strong letters of recommendation. All of the new hires reported to Daniel Kemp. All of them quit their jobs within a year of being hired. Dawn St. Claire, the vice-president of human resources, was shocked that all the new hires quit, so she contacted them to learn their reasons for quitting. They all suggested that their job positions lacked motivation. When Dawn told Daniel about these responses, he replied, "We paid them well. That should be enough motivation."

(1) Motivation Decision. Daniel Kemp suggests that Players Company should hire a motivational speaker for a day after it hires its next batch of managers. Do you think this will motivate the managers?

A motivational speaker will not solve the problem in a workplace in which employees are not given sufficient motivation to perform.

(2) Obtaining Employee Feedback. Once new entry-level managers are hired, Dawn St. Claire plans to meet with Daniel Kemp frequently to determine how the new managers are performing. Will this strategy solve the lack of motivation of the new managers?

Dawn should meet directly with the new managers, because Daniel may be an ineffective manager and meetings with him will not necessarily solve the problem of the managers' lack of motivation. The employees will have a chance to express their concerns, which could lead Dawn to devise better ways to motivate the employees.

(3) Discipline as Motivation. Dawn prefers not to discipline Daniel Kemp for his management style because she believes that Daniel would be upset if she told him that he needs to change. What is the problem if Dawn ignores Daniel's poor management style?

If Dawn ignores his management style, the next batch of managers who are hired may become dissatisfied with Daniel and will quit.

(4) Empowerment as Motivation. Dawn St. Claire has decided that the employees should set workplace policies to ensure that they will be motivated. Are there any disadvantages to letting employees have this much power?

The employees may establish policies that reward themselves excessively. However, the firm could at least let them propose policies, and it could decide to implement only those policies that it believes will improve the motivation of employees.

Web Insight — How Google Motivates Employees

At the opening of the chapter, Google was introduced. Go to the website (www.google.com) and go to the sections describing what it is like to work at Google. (You can also obtain this information by inserting the search term "Google Jobs" on a search engine.) Review the information about the work environment at Google. Identify the main features that in your opinion would make Google a great place to work.

Google makes an effort to ensure that employees like the work environment. Its workplace allows for much interaction among employees, and employees may be more willing to stay at work if they really enjoy it. Some of Google's workplace features include its exercise facilities, game room, and cafeteria.

Dell's Secret for Success

Go to Dell's website (www.dell.com) and click on the link "About Dell," near the bottom of the web page. You can also review a recent annual report of Dell for more information.

(1) Motivation. Explain how Dell's treatment of its employees motivates them to perform well.

Dell has established leadership programs for its employees, so that they develop leadership skills. This may make them enjoy their job, and perform better.

(2) Employee Rewards. Dell sometimes promotes some of its employees rather than hiring higher-level employees from other firms. Why is this beneficial?

Dell can reward its best employees by promoting them and is more likely to keep its best employees when using this process.

Video Exercise — Lessons in Employee Motivation

Many free business videos are available on websites such as YouTube (www.youtube.com), and more are added every day. Search for a recent video clip about an existing business that offers lessons on "employee motivation" in YouTube or any other website that provides video clips.

(1) Main Lesson. What is the name of the business in the video clip? Is the video clip focused on motivating the executives, or motivating the other employees, or some other aspect of employee motivation? What is the main lesson of the video clip that you watched?

Answers will vary among students. The main point is to ensure that students take the initiative to access and watch a related video and recognize the main lesson provided by the video.

(2) Trusting Employees. Some related videos suggest that an entrepreneur can improve the motivation of employees by trusting them. What does this mean?

If entrepreneurs trust their employees, they give the employees more responsibilities, and the employees are willing to work harder under these conditions.

(3) Motivation Methods. What methods of motivation are suggested in the video clip that you watched? For example, does the business advocate high compensation, empowerment, job security, a flexible work schedule, or employee involvement programs?

Answers will vary among students. The point is for students to apply what they watched to the concepts in the text.

Chapter 11: Hiring, Training, and Evaluating Employees

Introduction

The **Learning Objectives** for this chapter are to:

1. Explain human resource planning by firms.

2. Explain how a firm can ensure equal opportunity and the benefits of doing so.

3. Differentiate among the types of compensation that firms offer to employees.

4. Describe the skills of employees that firms develop.

5. Explain how the performance of employees can be evaluated.

1. Human Resource Planning
Human resource planning is the act of planning to satisfy a firm's needs for employees. It consists of three tasks.

1.1 Forecasting Staffing Needs
Since it is impossible to forecast how many workers will quit or how fast the business will grow with perfect accuracy, forecasting human resource needs is not an exact science.

1.2 Job Analysis
- A job specification states the credentials necessary for a specific position.
- A job description states the tasks and responsibilities of the position.

1.3 Recruiting
Recruiting ensures that the firm has an adequate supply of qualified candidates for employment.
- Internal recruiting — seeks qualified individuals within the firm
- External recruiting — attracts applicants from outside the firm
- Screening process:
  - Application — assessed to screen out candidates who lack the background, education and experience to qualify for the job
  - Interview process — assess the personality, promptness, attitude, and communications skills
  - References — may be of limited use as most references provide only favorable information

- o Employment tests — measure job-related skills or assess the candidate's ability to work well with others
- o Physical examination — determines whether the candidate is physically capable of doing the work, and may also include drug tests
- o Hiring decision — firm offers the job to the top candidate. If this candidate does not accept the offer, other qualified candidates can be considered.

2. Providing Equal Opportunity

2.1 Federal Laws Related to Discrimination
- The Equal Pay Act of 1963
- The Civil Rights Act of 1964
- The Age Discrimination in Employment Act of 1967
- The Americans with Disabilities Act (ADA) of 1990
- The Civil Rights Act of 1991

2.2 Diversity Incentives
Diversity can benefit firms in three ways:
- Studies have shown that employees who work in a more diverse workplace tend to be more innovative.
- Employees in a diverse workplace are more likely to understand different points of view and are capable of interacting with a diverse set of customers.
- The proportion of a firm's customer base that consists of minorities will continue to increase.

3. Compensation Packages That Firms Offer
A compensation package is the total monetary compensation and benefits offered to employees. It has several components.

3.1 Salary (or wages)

3.2 Stock Options — allow employees to buy the firm's stock at a specified price. This can motivate employees to maximize the firm's value and stock price. However, stock options can tempt managers to manipulate financial statements.

3.3 Commissions — compensation for meeting specific sales objectives

3.4 Bonuses — extra one-time payments at the end of a period in which employee performance is measured

3.5 Profit Sharing — returns a portion of the firm's profits back to the employees

3.6 Employee Benefits — paid vacations, health and life insurance, and pension programs

3.7 Perquisites ("perks") — include a company car, free parking, membership at clubs, and an expense account

3.8 Comparison Across Jobs

4. **Developing Skills of Employees**
Firms provide training to develop a variety of skills needed by their employees.

4.1 Technical Skills — needed to do daily tasks

4.2 Decision-Making Skills — to make better decisions and generate new ideas

4.3 Customer Service Skills — to interact with customers

4.4 Safety Skills — can reduce medical and legal expenses

4.5 Human Relations Skills — to assure employees are treated fairly and with respect

5. **Evaluation of Employee Performance**

Employee evaluations are used to help allocate raises and bonuses, provide feedback and direction to employees, and determine who qualifies for promotions.

5.1 Segmenting the Evaluation
- Objective versus subjective

5.2 Using a Performance Evaluation Form

5.3 Assigning Weights to Criteria

5.4 Steps for Proper Evaluation
- Communicate job responsibilities.
- Inform employees of their deficiencies.
- Be consistent in treatment of employees.

5.5 Action Due to Performance Evaluation
- Employees with favorable evaluations deserve to be recognized.
- When employees have poor evaluations, determine the cause. The appropriate action depends on the reason for the problem and the willingness and ability of the employee to correct it.
- Communicate deficiencies in the employee's evaluation and allow the employee a chance to respond.

5.6 Dealing with Lawsuits by Fired Employees

5.7 Employee Evaluation of Supervisors

Appendix: Labor Unions

A1. Background on Unions

A2. Negotiations Between Unions and Management

A3. Conflicts Between Unions and Management

Solutions to End-of-Chapter Exercises

Concept Review Questions

(1) Business Valuation. Explain why the hiring, training, and evaluation of employees can affect the value of a business.

Hiring good employees can increase productivity. Training employees properly can improve productivity. Proper evaluation of employees can motivate them and can help them improve. Overall, better employee productivity leads to higher sales (more revenue), better production efficiency (lower expenses), and therefore higher profits and a higher business valuation.

(2) Job Analysis. Explain what is involved in a job analysis.

Job analysis consists of developing:
- A job specification, which states the credentials necessary for a specific position.
- A job description, which states the tasks and responsibilities of the position.

(3) Recruiting. Describe the steps involved in the recruiting process:

- **Application** — assessed to screen out candidates who lack the background, education, and experience to qualify for the job
- **Interview process** — assesses the personality, promptness, attitude, and communications skills
- **References** — may be of limited use as most references provide only favorable information
- **Employment tests** — measure job-related skills or assess the candidate's ability to work well with others
- **Physical examination** — determines whether the candidate is physically capable of doing the work, and may also include drug tests

- **Hiring decision** — firm offers the job to the top candidate. If this candidate does not accept the offer, other qualified candidates can be considered.

(4) Internal Recruiting. What is the benefit of internal recruiting? What is a potential disadvantage of internal recruiting?

Internal recruiting is an effort to fill open positions with persons who are already employed by the firm. It can be beneficial because there is more information about the skills, abilities, and attitudes of existing employees. In addition, it offers an incentive to existing workers who want to be promoted.

A disadvantage of internal recruiting is that it may prevent the firm from hiring the most qualifed person for the job position, if the best qualified person is not already employed by the firm.

(5) Diversity. Describe the potential benefits to a firm that achieves diversity among its employees.

Diversity can benefit firms in three ways:
1. Studies have shown that employees who work in a more diverse workplace tend to be more innovative.
2. Employees in a diverse workplace are more likely to understand different points of view and are capable of interacting with a diverse set of customers.
3. The proportion of a firm's customer base that consists of minorities will continue to increase.

(6) Compensation Package. Describe the key components of a compensation package.

A compensation package represents the total monetary compensation and benefits offered to employees and consists of:
- Salary (or wages)
- Stock options — allow employees to buy the firm's stock at a specified price. This can motivate employees to maximize the firm's value and stock price. However, stock options can tempt managers to manipulate financial statements.
- Commissions — compensation for meeting specific sales objectives
- Bonus — extra one-time payment at the end of a period in which employee performance is measured
- Profit sharing — returns a portion of the firm's profits back to the employees
- Benefits — paid vacations, health and life insurance, and pension programs
- Perquisites ("perks") — include a company car, free parking, membership at clubs, and an expense account

(7) Stock Options. Explain how stock options can align the goals of managers and shareholders. Explain why stock options are not always an effective method of compensation.

Stock options provide a larger reward to managers when the stock price rises. So if the managers can make decisions that raise the price of the stock, they are rewarded directly. However, the stock price is determined by many factors, and managers may believe that they have no influence on the stock price. Thus, they would have no incentive to make decisions that enhance the firm's value if they think their decisions will not affect the value. Also, managers may be tempted to manipulate the financial statements to increase the stock price temporarily at the time that they plan to sell their stock holdings.

(8) Employee Skills. Explain the key work skills that are needed by human resources.

Firms provide training to develop a variety of skills needed by their employees.
- **Technical skills** — needed to do daily tasks
- **Decision-making skills** — to make better decisions and generate new ideas
- **Customer service skills** — to interact with customers
- **Safety skills** — can reduce medical and legal expenses
- **Human relations skills** — to assure employees are treated fairly and with respect

(9) Employee Evaluations. Explain the key steps of employee evaluations.

An employee evaluation is used to help allocate raises and bonuses, provide feedback and direction to employees, and determine who qualifies for promotions. The evaluation criteria can be objective or subjective. A performance evaluation form can be used to record the evaluation. Weights are assigned to the criteria. The supervisor should communicate the job responsibilities and the weights to be assigned to various criteria to the employees before the evaluation period begins. Once the evaluation period is over, the evaluation should be provided to employees, with feedback on any deficiencies and compliments where appropriate. For any negative evaluations, employees should be allowed a chance to respond.

(10) Upward Appraisals. What are upward appraisals? Why should firms encourage upward appraisals?

Upward appraisals are employee evaluations of their supervisors. Upward appraisals can indicate deficiencies in the supervisors that need to be corrected. In addition, feedback for supervisors on what they do well is also important. Overall, the feedback should help supervisors improve and do a better job of managing, which enhances productivity and employee morale.

Class Communication Questions

(1) Hiring Dilemma. A small business has 40 employees, and all six managers are males. The business wants to create more diversity by gender in its management. It currently has one managerial position open. Many of its existing employees quality for the position, and its top three internal applicants for this position are males. Should it hire a male applicant internally, hire a female applicant internally, or hire a female applicant who does not work for the business but whose qualifications are at least as high as those of any internal candidate?

Opinions will vary and this leads to interesting discussion. Whoever is not hired will likely claim that they were treated unfairly so there is no perfect solution, but this situation sometimes occurs in reality. The firm should have established some guidelines about hiring. If its guidelines state that it promotes employees internally if they qualify for a position, it should attempt to follow that guideline. However, it may also have some guidelines about achieving diversity. In some cases, attempting to achieve one guideline makes it impossible to achieve another guideline.

(2) Commission Dilemma. If you owned a small retail clothing store, would you pay your workers a commission based on how much clothing they sold? Is there a way that you could motivate them to sell, yet prevent them from giving bad advice to customers just to generate sales?

Commissions can motivate employees, but it may help to closely monitor returns by customers or complaints by customers that may indicate employees were too aggressive at selling the clothing.

(3) Labor Union Issue. Are labor unions (discussed in the appendix) beneficial to U.S. businesses?

Answers will vary and be dependent on the background of the student. Many students who have friends or family in unions will argue for them. The commonly cited advantages of a union are job security and high wages. However, some students will argue that since unions result in higher expenses for U.S. firms, U.S. consumers will prefer to buy products from foreign competitors.

Small Business Case — Hiring, Compensation, and Performance Evaluation Decisions

Web Czar Company develops websites for businesses. It recently received many orders from businesses that either want new websites or want to revise their existing websites. Brent Barber, the owner, forecasts that he needs to hire at least two more website designers on a full-time basis. He conducts a job analysis and develops job specification stating the credentials that the designers need. The job openings are posted in the local newspaper. Brent engages in external recruiting by reviewing all the applications on file and new applications that arrive in response to the posted job openings.

(1) Interviewing Decision. Brent would prefer to hire designers based on their credentials without conducting formal interviews. Why might this strategy backfire?

Even though the credentials on a résumé may be excellent, an applicant may not get along with other employees. An applicant's limited ability to get along with employees might be detected if interviewed by various employees.

(2) Screening Applicants. If many applicants have equally strong credentials, what characteristic could be used to select an applicant for a job?

The applicant's interaction with other employees is very important, as the ideal applicant might even improve the productivity of existing employees.

(3) Hiring from Within the Business. Some existing employees of Web Czar Company are upset with Brent because they want to be hired for the open job positions. They do not have the skills to be web designers, but they say that they have been loyal employees for more than five years and should be promoted to the position of web designer. Should Brent hire these employees for the web designer positions?

No. This hiring decision would backfire because these employees are not qualified for the job. The idea of hiring existing employees for open job positions is only appropriate if they are fully qualified.

(4) Performance Evaluation. The web designers of Web Czar Company are evaluated according to how well they satisfy the business's clients. The amount of time they spend on a web design project is not considered. Explain why the amount of time spent on a web design project deserves to be considered when assessing employee performance.

The amount of time spent on a web design project determines how many web design projects an employee may complete in a given month. This measures the speed of the work and should be considered along with the quality of the work.

Web Insight

At the opening of the chapter, PepsiCo was introduced. Go to the website (www.pepsico.com) and go to the section on Diversity. Summarize PepsiCo's comments about why it attempts to achieve diversity.

As a result of a diverse workforce, PepsiCo can relate to a diverse group of customers, and this may also help it understand the preferences of its customers. In addition, the diversity can make women and minorities more comfortable in the workplace, which may help to improve their productivity.

Dell's Secret for Success

Go to Dell's website (www.dell.com) and click on the link "About Dell," near the bottom of the web page. You can also review a recent annual report of Dell for more information.

(1) Diversity. Describe Dell's success in achieving a diverse workplace.

Many of Dell's employees are women and minorities. Many of its managers are women and minorities.

(2) Impact of Diversity. How do you think diversity has resulted in higher performance at Dell?

It creates diverse ideas due to diverse backgrounds and different perspectives, which can be useful when planning for the future.

(3) Stock Option Compensation. Do you think Dell benefits from providing options to buy its stock at a low price as partial compensation to employees?

Yes, because the employees are more willing to stick with a company if they really believe that their options will pay off over time.

Video Exercise — Lessons in Hiring Employees

Many free business videos are available on websites such as YouTube (www.youtube.com), and more are added every day. Search for a recent video clip about an existing business that offers lessons on "hiring employees" in YouTube or any other website that provides video clips.

(1) Main Lesson. What is the name of the business in the video clip? Is the video clip focused on the job description, the interviewing process, or some other aspect of the hiring process? What is the main lesson of the video clip that you watched?

Answers will vary among students. The main point is to ensure that students take the initiative to access and watch a related video and recognize the main lesson provided by the video.

(2) Attention to Hiring Process. Many videos suggest that the success of a business is highly dependent on its employees. Most businesses attempt to hire good employees, but some businesses are much better at it than others. Why do you think some businesses are better at hiring employees?

Some businesses take the hiring process more seriously. They realize the adverse effects of hiring bad employees, and they use a structure that conducts a thorough assessment of employees.

(3) Employee Attitude. Some videos suggest that the most important characteristic of an applicant is attitude. What does this really mean? How can attitude make a difference?

Attitude affects an employee's willingness to help meet the objectives of the business. Some employees are self-centered and are not focused on business objectives. These employees are less likely to perform well for the business.

Solutions to End-of-Part Exercises (Part IV)

Video on Managing a Business — Hiring the Best Employees

The Small Business Administration plays a very important role in helping many small businesses. Its website, which offers a wide range of services and information for small businesses, has a section called Delivering Success (www.sba.gov/tools/audiovideo/ deliveringsuccess/index.html) that provides video clips of small business success stories. Go to this website, and watch the video called "Hiring and Developing Employees" (total time of clip is 9 minutes, 15 seconds).

This video contains advice from three entrepreneurs of very successful small businesses. All the entrepreneurs emphasize that the success of a small business is highly dependent on the employees that are hired. The insight provided by the entrepreneurs is summarized below:

- Entrepreneurs should give their employees more responsibilities. This not only allows entrepreneurs to focus on bigger decisions, but it also makes the job more enjoyable for employees.

- Businesses should take corrective action toward employees who are not performing well.

- Businesses should spend much time in screening job applicants so that they are likely to hire the applicants who will be most effective.

- Businesses should devote considerable time to training their employees to make sure that the employees are well informed about the products that they are producing or selling.

- Some businesses can benefit from hiring prospective employees for a trial period, so that their abilities and attitudes can be more fully assessed.

- Employees need to have goals that are aligned with those of the business.

(1) Interaction Between Motivation and Compensation. Explain how employee motivation (Chapter 10) and compensation (Chapter 11) are indirectly related.

Employees can be given more responsibilities, which may motivate them to work harder. If they perform well with these extra responsibilities, they may deserve a higher level of compensation. The compensation along with the responsibilities may further motivate them, which results in stronger performance and higher compensation as a result.

(2) Interaction Between Job Enrichment Programs and Compensation Package. Explains how a firm's job enrichment program (Chapter 10) can affect the compensation package (Chapter 11) that it must offer in order to attract good employees.

106

If a firm offers a very desirable job enrichment program, it may attract good employees even if it offers average compensation levels. Other firms with less desirable job enrichment programs may have to offer higher compensation.

(3) Interaction Between Motivation and Credentials. Are businesses successful because they motivate employees (Chapter 10) or because they effectively screen their job applicants and hire the best employees?

Successful businesses need to motivate employees and properly screen job applicants. Good screening is not sufficient, because a good prospect might become a bad employee if not motivated. Proper motivation is not sufficient, because an employee who has weak job skills and a bad attitude may perform poorly even if the business attempts to motivate the employee by assigning many responsibilities.

Chapter 12: Creating and Pricing Products

Introduction

The **Learning Objectives** for this chapter are to:

1. Explain the product line, mix, and life cycle.

2. Identify the main factors that affect a product's target market.

3. Identify the steps involved in creating a new product.

4. Explain the common methods used to differentiate a product.

5. Identify the factors that influence the pricing decision.

6. Discuss other pricing decisions that a firm may make.

1. Background on Products

1.1 Product Line — group of related products or services offered by a single firm

1.2 Product Mix — combination of product lines offered by a single firm

1.3 Product Life Cycle
- Introduction phase — the initial period when attempts are made to inform consumers about the product
- Growth phase — sales volume of the product increases rapidly. Marketing is used to reinforce the product's features
- Maturity phase — sales volume levels off as a result of the competition
- Decline phase — period in which sales volume and profits decline

2. Identifying a Target Market

2.1 Factors That Affect the Size of a Target Market
- Demographics — characteristics about the population
- Geography — surfboards are sold near beaches, while snow tires are sold where the weather is cold
- Economic factors — inflation, interest rates, and unemployment can have a major impact on consumer demand
- **Social values** — influence consumer tastes and preferences

2.2 The Use of E-Marketing to Expand the Target Market
- E-marketing — using the Internet to execute the design, pricing, distribution, and promotion of products
- E-commerce — using electronic technology to conduct business transactions

The Internet also allows firms to target foreign markets.

3. **Creating New Products**

   3.1 Use of Marketing Research to Create Products — determines consumer preferences

   3.2 Use of Research and Development to Create Products — experiment with new ideas for products

   3.3 Steps Necessary to Create a New Product
   - Develop a product idea based on consumer preferences by monitoring consumer behavior
   - Assess the feasibility of the product idea — forecasted revenues must exceed the projected costs
   - Design and test the product to determine whether to proceed with the idea
   - Distribute and promote the product
   - Post-audit the new product

4. **Product Differentiation**
   Product differentiation is the effort by a firm to distinguish its products and services from competing products in a way that provides the firm with a competitive advantage.

   4.1 Unique Product Design — may result in superior product safety, reliability, convenience, or consumer satisfaction

   4.2 Unique Packaging — unbreakable, disposable, or recyclable packaging can help distinguish a firm's product from others

   4.3 Unique Branding — to distinguish the firm's products from others
   - Family versus individual branding
   - Producer versus store or generic brands

   4.4 Summary of Methods Used to Differentiate Products

5. Pricing Strategies

5.1 Pricing According to the Cost of Production — estimate the per-unit cost of production and then add a profit markup (**cost-based pricing**)

5.2 Pricing According to the Supply of Inventory — If inventory levels are above the desired levels, reduce prices.

5.3 Pricing According to Competitors' Prices
- Penetration pricing — set a lower price than those of competing products
- Defensive pricing — reduce the price to defend the firm's market share from a price decrease by a competitor
- Predatory pricing — set prices low enough to drive out new or potential competitors
- Prestige pricing — set a higher than competitive price to achieve a top-of-the-line image for the company's product among consumers

5.4 Example of Setting a Product's Price. Price per unit must exceed expected cost per unit
- Break-even point — the sales volume at which total revenue equals total cost. If sales are lower than the break-even point, the firm will incur losses.

5.5 Pricing Technology-Based Products — technology-based products need to be priced to account for the cost of investing in technology

6. Additional Pricing Decisions

6.1 Discounting — charge lower prices to consumers whose demand is more sensitive to price

6.2 Sales Prices — used to attract consumers who search for sales, and encourage them to buy other items while they are at the store

6.3 Credit Terms — provide financing for potential customers who otherwise might not have the cash available for immediate purchase

Solutions to End-of-Chapter Exercises

Concept Review Questions

(1) Business Valuation. Explain how the decisions regarding the creation and pricing of products can affect the value of a business.

The creation of products influences the product line or mix that is offered, and determines the revenue to be generated. The products that are created also influence the expenses involved in the production process. Thus, the creation of products affects revenue and expenses, and therefore affects the profits and value of the business.

(2) Product Line Versus Mix. Explain the difference between a product line and a product mix.

The product line is a group of related products or services offered by a single firm. The product mix is the combination of product lines offered by a single firm.

(3) Product Life Cycle. Describe the phases of the product life cycle.

The product life cycle consists of the following phases:
- Introduction phase — the initial period when attempts are made to inform consumers about the product
- Growth phase — sales volume of the product increases rapidly. Marketing is used to reinforce the product's features
- Maturity phase — sales volume levels off as a result of the competition
- Decline phase — period in which sales volume and profits decline

(4) Target Market. Explain the factors that affect the size of the target market.

The size of a target market is influenced by:
- Demographics — characteristics about the population
- Geography — surfboards are sold near beaches, while snow tires are sold where the weather is cold
- Economic factors — inflation, interest rates, and unemployment can have a major impact on consumer demand
- Social values — influence consumer tastes and preferences

(5) e-Marketing. Explain how e-marketing can be used by a firm to expand its target market.

E-marketing is the use of the Internet to execute the design, pricing, distribution, and promotion of products. A firm could establish a website to accept orders and payment online from customers anywhere, including in foreign markets. The website can allow firms to receive orders at lower costs and to expand the target market. In addition, the website can be used to enhance a firm's distribution and its promotion of products.

(6) New Product. Describe the steps necessary to create a new product.

The steps to create a new product are:
- Develop a product idea — based on consumer preferences by monitoring consumer behavior
- Assess the feasibility of the product idea — forecasted revenues must exceed the projected costs

- Design and test the product to determine whether to proceed with idea
- Distribute and promote the product
- Post-audit the new product

(7) Product Differentiation. Explain how a firm can differentiate its product.

Product differentiation is the effort by a firm to distinguish its products and services from competing products in a way that provides the firm with a competitive advantage. A firm can differentiate its product by using:
- Unique design — may result in superior product safety, reliability, convenience, or consumer satisfaction
- Unique packaging — unbreakable, disposable, or recyclable packaging can help distinguish a firm's product from others
- Unique branding — to distinguish products from others

(8) Cost-Based Pricing. Compare cost-based pricing with setting the price of products in response to changes in inventories.

To use cost-based pricing, a firm determines its cost per unit of producing a product and then adds a markup. If inventories become too large, a firm can attempt to reduce inventories of any products by setting relatively low prices for them. This will result in a higher quantity demanded, which should reduce the inventories.

(9) Pricing Response to Competitors. Explain how a firm may price a product in response to prices of competitor's products.

A firm may use:
- Penetration pricing — set a lower price than those of competing products
- Defensive pricing — reduce the price to defend the firm's market share from a price decrease by a competitor
- Predatory pricing — set prices low enough to drive out new or potential competitors
- Prestige pricing — set a higher than competitive price to achieve a top-of-the-line image for the company's product among consumers

(10) Other Pricing Decisions. Explain the decisions to use discounting, sales prices, or credit terms for products.

A firm may use discounting in order to charge lower prices to consumers whose demand is more sensitive to price. It may set sales prices for some products in order to attract consumers who search for sales, and this encourages them to buy other items while they are shopping. A firm provides financing for potential customers who otherwise might not have the cash available for immediate purchase.

Class Communication Questions

(1) Target Market Dilemma. If you open a clothing store at the local mall, do you think your target market should be children, teenagers, consumers older than age 20, or all age groups?

A logical answer is to first determine which market has much demand for clothing and is not subject to excessive competition. A store has a better chance for success if it provides clothing that is in demand by many consumers and if the store does not face too much competition from other stores in the mall or nearby.

(2) Product Versus Pricing. Assume that you work in a clothing store and that your task is to increase the sales to students at your college. Do you think the product (type of clothing, brand name) or the price would be the key factor that influences the demand for the clothing?

Some students will argue that price is the most critical factor that influences the demand. However, some people are willing to pay higher prices for a particular brand. The answer depends on the consumer.

(3) Pricing Dilemma. A famous pro basketball player is about to launch new basketball shoes. The price must be at least $50 to cover the expenses of producing the shoes. Do you think the revenue from selling the shoes will be highest if the shoes are sold at your local mall for $50, $70, or $90?

Answers may vary. Some students may argue that a higher price could result in just as many sales because some consumers may only want expensive shoes, or they may think higher priced shoes are of better quality.

Small Business Case — Product Decisions

NightLife Film Company is a movie production firm that wants to expand its product offerings. It has a good reputation for producing science fiction films. It could expand its product line by offering new types of science fiction films that might appeal to different age groups. Another possibility is to produce comedies or other types of films. It must also decide how to expand its product mix. It currently produces films for theaters and sells DVDs of the films several months after they have been in theaters.

(1) Product Line Decision. What would be an advantage to NightLife Film Company if it keeps its product line focused on science fiction films?

It already has a good reputation in the science fiction area, and it could continue to focus on what it does well.

(2) Product Line Tradeoff. What would be a disadvantage to NightLife Film Company if it keeps its product line focused on science fiction films?

There could be a general decline in interest in science fiction films over time. The firm may benefit from diversifying its product line, so it is not adversely affected by changes in the types of movies that consumers desire.

(3) Target Market Decision. NightLife Film Company recently produced a new movie. It needs to advertise this movie to consumers. Why must it decide on its target market for this movie before it advertises the movie?

The advertising decisions are dependent on the target market because it needs to use advertising that will appeal to the target market. Therefore, it must decide on the target market before it decides how to advertise.

(4) Impact of Customer Feedback. NightLife Film Company commonly allows consumers to complete an online survey about any of its movies. Why may this feedback be useful, even though the movies have already been produced and cannot be changed?

The feedback may allow it to improve the production of new movies in a manner that would satisfy customers to a greater degree.

Web Insight — Product Differentiation at Apple

At the opening of the chapter, Apple was introduced. Go to Apple's website (www.apple.com) and go to a section where you can view the products. Select any product and review its description. Summarize Apple's comments about that product and how that product is differentiated from those produced by competitors.

Apple continually creates new products. Many of them are improvements of its existing products. The products commonly allow customers more convenience than other competing products.

Dell's Secret for Success

Go to Dell's website (www.dell.com) and click on the link "About Dell," near the bottom of the web page. You can also review a recent annual report of Dell to obtain more information.

(1) Target Market. Describe Dell's target markets.

Dell's target markets include business customers that buy computer systems, schools that buy computers for their students, and individual students.

(2) Product Line. How has Dell expanded its products?

Dell has expanded its products to include printers, digital movie players, and handheld computers.

(3) Product Line Expansion. Why do you think Dell benefited from expanding its products to include printers?

Dell has great name recognition and is trusted for its production of computers. Consumers who like Dell's computers may desire printers to be produced by Dell.

Video Exercise — Lessons in Creating New Products

Many free business videos are available on websites such as YouTube (www.youtube.com), and more are added every day. Search for a recent video clip about an existing business that offers lessons on "creating new products" in YouTube or any other website that provides video clips.

(1) Main Lesson. What is the name of the business in the video clip? Is the video clip focused on the skills needed to create a new product, or the technical applications of creating a new product, or the typical profile of entrepreneurs who create new products? What is the main lesson of the video clip that you watched?

Answers will vary among students. The main point is to ensure that students take the initiative to access and watch a related video and recognize the main lesson provided by the video.

(2) Constructive Criticism. Some related videos suggest that the first step in creating a new product is to determine what you do not like about an existing product. What does this mean?

If you find a deficiency in an existing product, there are other customers who probably also recognize that deficiency. If you could create a product that does not have this deficiency, you may satisfy customers. Thus, the first step is to identify the deficiency and then determine if you have the skills to fix the deficiency.

(3) Impact of Pricing. Some related videos suggest that a business should determine the price range of a new product before the product is fully developed, even though the total cost of production is not yet clear. Why?

A new product may be feasible only if it can be priced at or below the prices of other similar products that are already in the market. The price is also partially dependent on the cost of production. If the cost of the production is so high that the price would be much higher than other existing products in the market, it is not feasible to create this new product (unless its quality is much higher than the quality of existing products).

Chapter 13: Distributing Products

Introduction

The **Learning Objectives** for this chapter are to:

1. Explain the advantages and disadvantages of a direct channel of distribution, and identify factors that could determine the optimal channel of distribution.

2. Differentiate between types of market coverage.

3. Describe the various forms of transportation used to distribute products.

4. Explain how the distribution process can be accelerated.

5. Describe the characteristics of retailers.

6. Explain how wholesalers can serve manufacturers and retailers.

7. Explain the strategy and potential benefits of vertical channel integration.

1. Channels of Distribution

A **distribution channel** is the path a good follows from the producer to the consumer.

1.1 Direct Channel — producer deals directly with customers, without using intermediaries

- Advantages of a direct channel:
  - Producer receives the full difference between the manufacturer's cost and the price charged to the customer.
  - Producer has full control over the price to be charged to the customer.
  - Producer obtains firsthand feedback from customers.
- Disadvantages of a direct channel
  - Producer must perform all of the distribution functions itself, so it must incur the cost of more employees.
  - Producer that deals directly with customers may have to sell on credit.

1.2 One-Level Channel — one marketing intermediary is between the producer and the customer.

- **Merchants** become owners of the products and resell them.
- **Agents** match buyers and sellers without assuming ownership of the goods they help distribute.

1.3 Two-Level Channel — has two marketing intermediaries between the producer and the customer

1.4 Comparison of Distribution Systems

1.5 Factors That Determine the Optimal Channel of Distribution
- Ease of transporting the product — products that can be easily transported are more likely to involve intermediaries in the distribution channel
- Degree of standardization — standardized products are more likely to involve intermediaries in their distribution channels
- Reliance on Internet (website) — firms that sell via the Internet tend to use a direct channel since their websites are substitutes for retail stores

2. **Selecting the Degree of Market Coverage**
Market coverage is the degree of product distribution among outlets.

2.1 Intensive Distribution — the product is sold through as many outlets as possible. Examples include newspapers, cigarettes, soft drinks, candy, and chewing gum.

2.2 Selective Distribution — limits the number of outlets in which the product will be sold in order to ensure that the sellers have the necessary expertise to sell the product. Examples include computer equipment and quality clothing.

2.3 Exclusive Distribution — the product is sold in only one or a few outlets in a given area to create a perception of prestige for the product

2.4 Selecting the Optimal Type of Market Coverage

3. **Selecting the Transportation Used to Distribute Products**

3.1 Truck — most commonly used mode of transportation. Trucks can reach almost any destination relatively quickly and can make several stops on a single route.

3.2 Rail — most efficient mode when transporting heavy products over long distances. But rail transportation does not reach as many destinations as trucks.

3.3 Air — useful for small, light items, such jewelry and computer components.

3.4 Water — used to deliver bulk products across countries

3.5 Pipeline — used to deliver oil, natural gas, and coal

4. How to Accelerate the Distribution Process

4.1 Streamline the Channel of Distribution — eliminates part of the distribution network, such as warehouses

4.2 Use the Internet for Distribution — allows customers to more easily reach producers and reduces the need for intermediaries

4.3 Integrate the Production and Distribution Processes — if production process is poor, a firm cannot distribute enough product to satisfy demand no matter how efficient its distribution system is. By comparing orders (from the distribution process) to inventory (from the production process), the firm can anticipate future inventory shortages and adjust production to prevent shortages.

5. Characteristics of Retailers
Retailers can be described by the following characteristics:

5.1 Number of Outlets
- Independent retail store — has only one outlet
- Chain — has more than one outlet

5.2 Quality of Service
- Full-service retail store — offers sales assistance
- Self-service retail store — offers little or no sales assistance or service

5.3 Variety of Products Offered
- Specialty retail stores — focus on a narrow range of related products
- Variety retail stores — such as Sears and J.C. Penney offer wide variety of products

5.4 Store Versus Nonstore
- Mail-order retailers — receive orders by mail or over the phone and ship products through the mail
- Websites — for example, Amazon.com has become a major seller of books, videos, and other items without having any stores
- Vending machines — placed in many locations and accessible at all hours

6. Services Offered by Wholesalers

6.1 How Wholesalers Serve Manufacturers
- Warehousing — wholesalers buy items from manufacturers in bulk and hold them in their own warehouses, which reduces the amount of space manufacturers need for storage and the amount of money invested in maintaining inventories

- Sales expertise — wholesalers can use their expertise in selling the manufacturer's goods to retailers
- Delivery to retailers — wholesalers can simplify the shipping and delivery of goods, as manufacturers can transport products in bulk to the wholesaler
- Assumption of credit risk — wholesalers may allow retailers to use credit so that the manufacturer does not need to offer credit to retailers
- Information — wholesalers can provide feedback to manufacturers about retail pricing, displays, etc.

6.2 How Wholesalers Serve Retailers
- Warehousing — wholesalers store large quantities of products so that they can accommodate requests of retailers quickly
- Promotion — wholesalers may promote the products they distribute, which can increase sales by retailers
- Displays — wholesalers may set up displays to attract the attention of customers without using too much of the retailer's limited space
- Credit — wholesalers often sell goods on credit to retailers, providing the retailers with a form of shor-term financing
- Information — wholesalers can provide information about the pricing, promotion, hours, and special offers of other retailers

7. Vertical Channel Integration

7.1 Vertical Channel Integration by Manufacturers
A producer may establish its own retail stores. Before doing so, it must address the following questions:
- Can it absorb the additional costs of leasing store space and hiring workers to staff the retail outlets?
- Can it make full use of the store?
- Will the additional revenue from the stores be sufficient to cover the additional costss incurred?
- Will it lose the business it has developed with other outlets once it begins to compete at the retail level?

7.2 Vertical Channel Integration by Retailers
A retailer may produce its own products. Before doing so, it must address the following questions:
- Can it absorb the additional expenses associated with acquiring the plant, equipment, and employees?
- Does it have the expertise to adjust the production process as consumer tastes change over time?

Solutions to End-of-Chapter Exercises

Concept Review Questions

(1) Impact of Distribution on Business Valuation. Explain how distribution decisions of a firm can enhance its performance and value.

A firm must determine the route from the point at which it produces products until the products are sold to consumers. Some routes may be more effective than others. Thus, a firm that makes proper distribution decisions may be able to increase its sales and therefore increase revenue. In addition, it could possibly reduce its expenses if it uses the proper distribution channel.

(2) Direct Channel. Explain the advantages and disadvantages of direct channel distribution.

Advantages of a direct channel include:
- Producer receives the full difference between the manufacturer's cost and the price charged to the customer.
- Producer has full control over the price to be charged to the customer.
- Producer obtains firsthand feedback from customers.

Disadvantages of a direct channel include:
- Producer must perform all of the distribution functions itself, so it must incur the cost of more employees.
- Producer that deals directly with customers may have to sell on credit.

(3) Merchants Versus Agents. Compare the role of merchants versus agents in the distribution process.

Merchants become owners of the products and resell them. **Agents** match buyers and sellers without assuming ownership of the goods they help distribute.

(4) Channels of Distribution. Explain the difference between a one-level channel and a two-level channel of distribution.

A one-level channel has one intermediary, such as a retailer. A two-level channel reflects two intermediaries, such as a wholesaler and a retailer.

(5) Optimal Channel. Describe the factors that determine the optimal channel of distribution for distributing a product.

The following factors should be considered when deciding the optimal channel of distribution:

- **Ease of transporting the product** — products that can be easily transported are more likely to involve intermediaries in the distribution channel.
- **Degree of standardization** — standardized products are more likely to involve intermediaries in their distribution channels.
- **Reliance on Internet (website)** — firms that sell via the Internet tend to use a direct channel since their websites are substitutes for retail stores.

(6) Market Coverage. Describe the different types of market coverage that can be used by firms that produce products.

Firms can consider:
- **Intensive distribution** — the product is sold through as many outlets as possible. Examples include newspapers, cigarettes, soft drinks, candy, and chewing gum.
- **Selective distribution** — limits the number of outlets in which the product will be sold in order to ensure that the sellers have the necessary expertise to sell the product. Examples include computer equipment and quality clothing.
- **Exclusive distribution** — the product is sold in only one or a few outlets in a given area to create a perception of prestige for the product.

(7) Methods of Transportation. List the common methods of transporting products.

- **Trucks** — most commonly used mode of transportation. Trucks can reach almost any destination relatively quickly and can make several stops on a single route.
- **Railroads** — most efficient mode when transporting heavy products over long distances. But rail transportation does not reach as many destinations as trucks.
- **Air** — useful for small, light items, such jewelry and computer components.
- **Water** — used to deliver bulk products across countries.
- **Pipelines** — used to deliver oil, natural gas, and coal.

The optimal mode of transportation depends on the product.

(8) Accelerating Distribution. Explain how to accelerate the distribution process.

- Streamline the channel of distribution in order to eliminate part of the distribution network, such as warehouses.
- Integrate the production and distribution processes — if the production process is poor, a firm cannot distribute enough producs to satisfy demand no matter how efficient its distribution system is. By comparing orders (from the distribution process) to inventory (from the production process), the firm can anticipate future inventory shortages and adjust production to prevent shortages.

(9) Retailer Characteristics. Identify the various characteristics that can be used to describe retailers.

Retailers can be described by the following characteristics:

Number of outlets:
- Independent retail store — has only one outlet
- Chain — has more than one outlet

Quality of service
- Full-service retail store — offers sales assistance
- Self-service retail store — offers little or no sales assistance or service

Variety of products offered
- Specialty retail stores — focus on a narrow range of related products
- Variety retail stores — such as Sears and J.C. Penney offer wide variety of products
- Specialty stores — offer a certain degree of prestige

Store versus nonstore
- Mail-order retailers — receive orders by mail or over the phone and ship products through the mail
- Websites — for example, Amazon.com has become a major seller of books, videos, and other items without having any stores.
- Vending machines — placed in many locations and accessible at all hours

(10) Vertical Integration. If a manufacturer of a product considers vertical integration, what questions must the firm address to determine whether it is worthwhile?

Vertical channel integration by a manufacturer implies that the producer establishes its own retail stores. It must address the following questions:
- Can it absorb the additional costs of leasing store space and hiring workers to staff the retail outlets?
- Can it make full use of the store?
- Will the additional revenue from the stores be sufficient to cover the additional costss incurred?
- Will it lose the business it had developed with other outlets once it begins to compete at the retail level?

Class Communication Questions

(1) Intensive Versus Selective Distribution. If you owned a business that produced electronic games, would you use intensive or selective distribution?

Selective distribution would likely be preferred because consumers would go to specific types of stores to buy electronic games.

123

(2) Intermediary Dilemma. When intermediaries of sporting goods are involved in the distribution process, the price of the product is higher to compensate for their services. Are the intermediaries necessary or should they be circumvented by the manufacturers?

Intermediaries can be circumvented only if the manufacturer wants to sell direct to consumers. It could attempt this using the Internet, but will likely experience a much lower sales level as a result.

(3) Retail Store Dilemma. A publisher of books that appealed only to scientists is attempting to determine its distribution strategy. Should it attempt to sell its books through retail book stores? What alternative method of distribution may be more appropriate?

Book stores will not want to use shelf space for books that appeal to only a small group of people. The publisher may attempt to sell its books through its website.

Small Business Case — Distribution Decisions by Lada Inc.

Lada, Inc., produces office supplies and used to sell them to wholesalers. The wholesalers would then sell the supplies to retailers at a price of about 40 percent more than what they paid Lada for the supplies. This year, Lada created a website so that it could receive orders directly from the retail stores that sell office supplies. It now ships the office supplies directly to the retail stores. It is able to offer the stores a lower price for its supplies than what these stores were paying when a wholesaler was involved. Consequently, the demand for its supplies has increased substantially. By eliminating the intermediary, Lada has been able to generate more sales and improve its performance.

(1) Disadvantage of Eliminating Wholesalers. What is the disadvantage to Lada, Inc., of dealing directly with retailers?

Lada Inc., has to maintain its own inventory now, and it can no longer rely on wholesalers for promotion, displays, or credit granted to retailers. Thus, it could lose some sales that a wholesaler would have generated.

(2) Advantage of Eliminating Wholesalers. What is the advantage to Lada, Inc., of dealing directly with retailers?

Lada, Inc., can avoid the high markup in price that resulted when wholesalers were selling its product to retailers.

(3) Market Coverage. Why might Lada, Inc.,be able to reach more retail stores across the United States with its new distribution system?

The wholesalers that served Lada, Inc., in the past might not have reached all retail stores that sell office supplies. Lada now can reach all stores with its website, but it must consider methods to ensure that these stores are aware of its website.

Web Insight — Urban Outfitters' Reliance on Producers

At the opening of the chapter, Urban Outfitters was introduced. Go to www.urbanoutfitters.com and review the types of clothes that are available. Summarize what you learn from a quick review of clothes that you might consider purchasing. Specifically, does the store rely on one producer of clothing or many producers?

> The store relies on many different producers.

Dell's Secret for Success

Go to Dell's website (www.dell.com) and click on the link "About Dell," near the bottom of the web page. You can also review a recent annual report for more information.

(1) Distribution System. Review Dell's comments about its distribution. How does it distribute its products to its customers?

> Dell's main business is to sell directly to customers, so it avoids the intermediaries and has control of the price that customers pay for its products.

(2) Direct Channel. Describe the advantages of Dell's direct channel of distribution. What is a possible disadvantage of Dell's distribution system?

> Dell's distribution system ensures that customers are charged a low price. A disadvantage is that some consumers who rely on retailers may not be exposed to Dell's products.

(3) Website Sales. Dell has had success with its website sales. Why is Dell's website so important for its particular type of business?

> Dell relies on its website as a form of advertising. The website is important for distribution because consumers can order products directly from the website.

Video Exercise — Lessons in Distributing Products

Many free business videos are available on websites such as YouTube (www.youtube.com), and more are added every day. Search for a recent video clip about an existing business that offers lessons on "distributing products" in YouTube or any other website that provides video clips.

(1) Main Lesson. What is the name of the business in the video clip? Is the video clip focused on the type of market coverage, the transportation used to distribute the products, accelerating the distribution process, or some other aspect of entrepreneurship? What is the main lesson of the video clip that you watched?

Answers will vary among students. The main point is to ensure that students take the initiative to access and watch a related video and recognize the main lesson provided by the video.

(2) Reliance onWholesalers. Some videos explain the benefits of wholesaling. Based on the pros and cons of using a wholesaler, do you think the business in the video you watched relies on wholesalers?

Answers will vary among students, depending on the characteristics of the company that they learned about. Some companies can more easily reach retailers or consumers on their own and therefore would not need to rely on wholesalers.

(3) Reliance on Retailers. Some videos explain the benefits of retailing. Based on the pros and cons of using a retailer, do you think the business in the video you watched relies on retailers?

Answers will vary among students, depending on the characteristics of the company that they learned about. Some companies can more easily reach consumers on their own and therefore would not need to rely on retailers.

Chapter 14: Promoting Products

Introduction

The **Learning Objectives** for this chapter are to:

1. Explain how promotion can benefit firms.

2. Describe how advertising is used.

3. Describe the steps involved in personal selling.

4. Describe the sales promotion methods that are used.

5. Describe how firms can use public relations to promote products.

6. Explain how firms select the optimal mix of promotions to use.

1. **Benefits of Promotion**
   Promotion is the act of informing or reminding consumers about a specific good or service. It can enhance sales.

   1.1 Promotion Mix — the combination of methods that a firm uses to increase the acceptance of its products in the marketplace. The four methods of promotion are (1) advertising, (2) personal selling, (3) sales promotion, and (4) public relations.

2. **Advertising**
   Advertising — is a paid, nonpersonal sales presentation communicated through various media or nonmedia forms to influence a large number of consumers

   2.1 Reasons for Advertising
   - Brand advertising — enhance the image of a specific brand
   - Comparative advertising — demonstrates a brand's superiority by comparison with other competing brands
   - Reminder advertising — helps consumers remember the product's existence
   - Institutional advertising — enhances the image of a specific institution (commonly conducted by utility firms)
   - Industry advertising — enhances the image of a specific industry (milk)

   2.2 Forms of Advertising
   - Newspapers — reaches a particular geographic area

- Magazines — can reach large national markets or selected special interest groups
- Radio — lacks a visual effect, but can reach a particular target market
- Television — reaches a large audience
- Internet — popular means of advertising. Banner ads appear at the top of a web page. Button ads take the viewer to the website of the firm that placed the ad if the viewer clicks on the ad
- e-mail — some e-mail promotions are personalized to fit customer interests, whereas others are general and apply to all customers on a firm's e-mail list
- Direct mail — can reach a specific target market
- Telemarketing — utilizes the telephone for promoting and selling products and services
- Outdoor ads — billboards and signs
- Transportation ads — mounted on buses and taxi cabs
- Specialty ads — include nonmedia advertising such as T-shirts and bumper stickers

3. Personal Selling

3.1. Identify the Target Market — determine the type of consumers who may be interested in the product

3.2 Contact Potential Customers

3.3 Make the Sales Presentation — explain how the product or service can satisfy customer needs

3.4 Answer Questions

3.5 Close the Sale

3.6 Follow Up — this effort increases the credibility of the salespeople and opens the door for additional business.

3.7 Managing Salespeople

4. Sales Promotion

Sales Promotion — is a set of activities that is intended to influence consumers to buy a particular good or service

4.1 Rebates — potential refunds by the manufacturer directly to the consumer

4.2 Coupons — used in newspapers, magazines, and ads to encourage the purchase of a product

4.3 Sampling — the act of offering free samples to entice consumers to try a new brand or product

4.4 Displays

4.5 Premium — gift or prize provided free to consumers who purchase a specific product

4.6 Summary of Sales Promotion Strategies

5. **Public Relations**
Common types of public relations strategies:

5.1 Special Events — increase product awareness

5.2 News Releases — brief written announcements provided by the firm to the media

5.3 Press Conferences — oral announcements provided to the media

6. **Determining the Optimal Promotion Mix**

6.1 Target Market — if target market is a wide variety of consumers, advertising may be necessary
- Pull strategy — promotions directed specifically at the target market
- Push strategy — promotions directed at the wholesale or retail level

6.2 Promotion Budget
If the budget is small, a firm may have to rely on inexpensive sales promotion methods.

The promotion budget is dependent on:
- The firm's phase in the product life cycle
- The level of advertising used by the competition
- Changes in economic conditions

6.3 Evaluating and Revising a Firm's Promotions
Promotional programs should establish goals (sales volume, etc.), so that they can be evaluated based on whether the goals were achieved.

Solutions to End-of-Chapter Exercises

Concept Review Questions

(1) Impact of Promotion on Business Valuation. Explain how promotion strategies can enhance the performance and valuation of a business.

Promotion strategies can affect the volume of sales generated by the firm and therefore influence revenue. There is a cost of using promotion strategies, so firms that more effectively use promotion strategies may incur lower expenses for this purpose. Since promotion strategies affect a firm's revenue and expenses, they affect a firm's profits, performance, and value.

(2) Promotion Mix. Identify the key components of a firm's promotion mix.

A firm's promotion mix includes (1) advertising, (2) personal selling, (3) sales promotion, and (4) public relations.

(3) Reasons for Advertising. What are the common reasons for advertising?

Common methods for advertising are as follows:
- Brand advertising — enhances the image of a specific brand
- Comparative advertising — demonstrate a brand's superiority by comparison with other competing brands
- Reminder advertising — helps consumers remember the product's existence
- Institutional advertising — enhance the image of a specific institution (commonly conducted by utility firms)
- Industry advertising — enhances the image of a specific industry (milk)

(4) Forms of Advertising. What are the common forms of advertising?

Common forms of advertising are as follows:
- Newspapers — reach a particular geographic area
- Magazines — can reach large national markets or selected special interest groups
- Radio — lacks a visual effect, but can reach a particular target market
- Television — reaches a large audience
- Internet — popular means of advertising. Banner ads appear at the top of a web page. Button ads take the viewer to the website of the firm that placed the ad if the viewer clicks on the ad
- E-mail — some e-mail promotions are personalized to fit customer interests whereas others are general and apply to all customers on a firm's e-mail list
- Direct mail — can reach a specific target market
- Telemarketing — utilizes the telephone for promoting and selling products and services
- Outdoor ads — billboards and signs

- Transportation ads — mounted on buses and taxi cabs
- Specialty ads — include nonmedia advertising such as T-shirts and bumper stickers

(5) E-mail Advertisements. Why do you think e-mail advertisements have limited effectiveness?

Many consumers believe that e-mail advertisements are an invasion of privacy and will not read them.

(6) Sales Promotion Strategies. Identify commonly used sales promotion strategies.

Common sales promotion strategies include:
- Rebate — potential refund by the manufacturer directly to the consumer
- Coupons — used in newspapers, magazines, and ads to encourage the purchase of a product
- Sampling — the act of offering free samples to entice consumers to try a new brand or product
- Premium — gift or prize provided free to consumers who purchase a specific product

(7) Optimal Promotion Mix. Explain why the target market affects the optimal promotion mix. Explain why the promotion budget affects the optimal promotion mix.

The optimal promotion mix is dependent on the target market. If the target market represents a wide variety of consumers, advertising may be necessary. The promotion budget is the amount of funds set aside for promotion methods. If the budget is large, a firm can consider expensive forms of promotion such as advertising. However, if the promotion budget is small, a firm may have to rely on inexpensive sales promotion methods.

(8) Pull Versus Push Strategies. Explain the difference between a pull strategy and a push strategy.

A pull strategy reflects a promotion aimed directly at the target market. Consumers then become aware of the product and then request the product from retailers, who request it from wholesalers or producers. Thus, the product is pulled through the distribution channel as a result of consumer demand.

The push strategy is directed at wholesalers or retailers, who promote the product to retailers, and the retailers promote it to consumers. Thus, the push strategy pushes the product through the channels of distribution.

(9) Promotion Budget. Why is the promotion budget influenced by the product's present phase in the product life cycle?

When a product is introduced to the market, the promotion budget for that product needs to be large to make consumers aware of the product. In later phases of the product life cycle, the promotion budget can be smaller because consumers should already be aware of the product.

(10) Evaluating Promotion Strategies. How can firms evaluate the performance of a particular promotion strategy that they apply in a particular period?

Firms should set sales goals or other goals for a particular promotion strategy. After the period is over, they can compare the actual sales (or whatever) to the goal.

Class Communication Questions

(1) Target for Advertisements. If your business produces toys that are sold to children between the ages of five and ten years, would you advertise the product to the children or to their parents?

The correct answer depends on whether toy purchases are attributed to a parent decision or to requests from children. Many children will communicate their preferences to their parents. Many parents make toy purchases for children based on requests from the children.

.

(2) Promotion Dilemma. If you owned a retail store that sells electronic games, what would be an affordable and effective method of advertising you could use to increase your sales?

Local newspaper and direct mail are relatively inexpensive and could be effective to advertise a local store to customers within a given town.

(3) Internet Advertising Dilemma. Do you think that a retail store in the local mall would benefit from advertising on the main web page of Google or Yahoo?

This form of advertising would be very expensive because it reaches consumers throughout the United States. A local advertisement in a newspaper may reach just as many people in the local area and would not be as costly.

Small Business Case — Promotion Decisions

Karma Coffee Company was recently opened in downtown Boston. The owner, Stephanie Logan, wants to attract many of the people who work in major office complexes nearby. Stephanie is hoping that they will stop in Karma for coffee before they start work, after they leave work in the evening, or during breaks for informal meetings with business associates or friends. She decides that the local business people represent her target market.

(1) Spending Money for Promotion. Explain why Stephanie may benefit from spending money to promote her business.

Many people will not know about her business unless she advertises it.

(2) Advertising Decision. Television advertising reaches a very large audience, but it is very expensive. Would this form of advertising be worthwhile for Karma Coffee?

No. The coffee house needs to attract local business people and should not have to advertise on television just to reach the small group of people that may possibly go to the coffee house.

(3) Sales Presentation Advantage. Stephanie contacted the special events director of each firm in the vicinity of Karma Coffee in downtown Boston and made a sales presentation about how her coffee house may be the ideal place for their events. What is an advantage of personal selling over advertising?

Personal selling reaches people on a personal level, and they are able to ask questions.

(4) Sales Promotion Advantage. Stephanie decides to provide local business employees with brochures on her coffee house. Each brochure contains a coupon for a free coffee. What benefit does this sales promotion provide that Karma Coffee would not obtain from advertising?

The offer of free coffee in the sales promotion may attract some customers who would ignore advertising that does not include a coupon.

Web Insight — Coca Cola's Web Promotions

At the opening of the chapter, The Coca Cola Company was introduced. Go to the website (www.cocacola.com) and review a section that has promotions (such as the section called "Rewards"). Summarize the type of promotions that The Coca Cola Company uses on its website.

The Coca Cola Company commonly offers various types of premiums on its website.

Dell's Secret for Success

Go to Dell's website (www.dell.com) and click on the link "About Dell," near the bottom of the web page. You can also review a recent annual report for more information.

(1) Degree of Advertising. Dell does not use excessive advertising. It tends to use more of its funds to focus on high-quality production and customer satisfaction. Does this strategy make sense?

Yes. Also, if it uses more funds in production and service, it can achieve high quality, and the products will sell themselves.

(2) Product Life Cycle. Dell is beyond the introduction phase of the product life cycle. Why might Dell have to change its promotion strategy when it enters the decline phase of the product life cycle?

Dell may need to advertise more to prevent any loss in market share during the decline phase of the product life cycle.

Video Exercise — Lessons in Promotion

Many free business videos are available on websites such as YouTube (www.youtube.com), and more are added every day. Search for a recent video clip about an existing business that offers lessons on "promotion" in YouTube or any other website that provides video clips.

(1) Main Lesson. What is the name of the business in the video clip? Is the video clip focused on the firm's use of advertising, its personal selling, sales promotion methods, public relations, or some other aspect of promotion? What is the main lesson of the video clip that you watched?

> Answers will vary among students. The main point is to ensure that students take the initiative to access and watch a related video and recognize the main lesson provided by the video.

(2) Benefits of Public Relations. Some entrepreneurs say that they attempt to interact with customers every chance they get, regardless of the event. Why?

> Entrepreneurs want to ensure that their business is widely recognized by the local customers. Their interaction with the local customers is a method of reminder advertising, in which the customer is continually reminded about that business.

(3) Ideal Method of Advertising. Some businesses mention in videos that direct mail is their ideal method of advertising. Yet, other businesses say that radio or television is their ideal method of advertising. Who is right?

> The ideal method can vary among businesses depending on their characteristics, such as whether their customers are in one community, or spread across the U.S.

Solutions to End-of-Part Exercises (Part V)

Video on Managing a Business — Marketing for Success

The Small Business Administration plays a very important role in helping many small businesses. Its website, which offers a wide range of services and information for small businesses, has a section called Delivering Success (www.sba.gov/tools/audiovideo/deliveringsuccess/index.html) that provides video clips of small business success stories. Go to this website, and watch the video called "Planning and Research" (total time of clip is 6 minutes, 40 seconds).

In this video clip, two entrepreneurs with their successful businesses summarize their marketing research experience. Many small businesses are not necessarily known by consumers. Therefore, marketing may be crucial for them. When determining the ideal marketing strategy to use, businesses should attempt to put themselves in the position of a consumer and assess how they would respond to the various advertising methods that could be applied. A business may initially experiment with various advertising methods and monitor the results to determine which method led the customers to the business. The marketing strategy of a small business can affect the key components of a business plan. The revenue of a business may be influenced by the marketing strategy, and the amount of financing that a business can obtain can be influenced by the estimated revenue.

(1) Interaction Between Target Market and Advertising Strategy. Explain how the marketing strategy (Chapter 14) of a small business is related to the target market identified by the business (Chapter 12).

The target market identifies the profile of the potential customers, such as where they live. The marketing strategy is dependent on the target market. If the target market is a neighborhood, the marketing strategy may include direct mail to a specific zip code. Alternatively, if the target market is throughout an entire city, a better marketing strategy may include radio advertising.

(2) Interaction Between Distribution and Advertising Methods. Explain how the distribution strategy (Chapter 13) and the marketing strategy (Chapter 14) of a small business are related.

If the distribution of products is through retailers, the marketing strategy may be more limited because consumers will see the products when they visit retail stores. Conversely, if the firm wants to sell the product directly to the consumer without an intermediary, it will need a marketing strategy that can inform consumers about the product.

(3) Interaction Between Pricing and Promotion. Explain how the pricing of a product (Chapter 12) is related to promotion (Chapter 14).

A small business prices its product in accordance with the image or prestige of the product. The promotion and advertising of the product should be consistent with that image or prestige. For example, prestige products that are priced relatively high are likely to rely on advertising methods that appeal to consumers in high income levels.

Chapter 15: Accounting and Financial Analysis

Introduction

The **Learning Objectives** for this chapter are to:

1. Explain how firms use accounting.

2. Explain how firms can ensure proper financial reporting.

3. Explain how to interpret financial statements.

4. Explain how to evaluate a firm's financial condition.

1. How Firms Use Accounting

1.1 Reporting
Reporting accurate data regarding the firm's financial transactions is the purpose of financial accounting.

- Reporting to investors — for publicly traded firms
- Reporting to creditors — lending institutions often require a firm's most recent financial statements so that they can assess the creditworthiness of the firm

1.2 Decision Support
Firms conduct managerial accounting to provide information internally to help managers make good decisions.

1.3 Control
By reviewing financial information, managers can monitor and control the performance of individuals, divisions, and products.

Auditing refers to the assessment of the records that were used to prepare the firm's financial statements.

Internal auditors specialize in evaluating the various divisions of a business to ensure that they are operating efficiently.

2. Responsible Financial Reporting

Firms have some flexibility in their accounting process. Thus, the financial statements may vary with the accounting method used, which means that financial statements might be manipulated to inflate earnings.

2.1 The Role of Auditors in Ensuring Proper Reporting — ensure that all information in a financial statement is accurate

2.2 The Role of Directors in Ensuring Proper Reporting

They can oversee the audit process to make sure that an auditor has no conflict of interests and will do an honest audit of the reporting process.

2.3 The Role of the Sarbanes-Oxley Act

Congress enacted this law to make corporate executives more accountable for the accuracy of financial statements. The Securities and Exchange Commission has been granted more resources and power to monitor financial reporting.

3. Interpreting Financial Statements

3.1 Income Statement — indicates the revenue, expenses, and profits (or losses) of a firm over a period of time

The components of an income statement are:
- Net sales — total sales adjusted for any discounts
- Cost of goods sold — the cost of all materials that were used to produce the goods that were sold
- Gross profit — equals net sales minus the cost of goods sold
- Operating expenses — composed of selling expenses as well as general and administrative expenses
- Earnings before interest and taxes (EBIT) — calculated by subtracting the firm's operating expenses from its gross profits
- Earnings before taxes — equal earnings before interest and taxes minus interest expenses
- Earnings after taxes, sometimes referred to as net income — equal earnings before taxes minus taxes

3.2 Balance Sheet — reports the book value of all assets, liabilities, and owner's equity of a firm at a given point in time. The relationship between the items on a balance sheet is described by the basic accounting equation:

Assets = Liabilities + Owner's Equity

- Assets represent anything of value owned by the firm

- o Current assets — will be converted into cash within one year. Examples include cash, marketable securities, accounts receivable, and inventories.
  - o Fixed assets — will be used by the firm for more than one year. Examples include the firm's plant and equipment. These assets are subject to depreciation, which represents a reduction in the value of a fixed asset to reflect deterioration.
- Liabilities are what the firm owes
  - o Current liabilities are due in a year or less. They include accounts payable, which represent money owed for the purchase of materials and supplies. Another current liability is notes payable, which are short-term loans from creditors.
  - o Long-term liabilities represent debts that will be paid later than one year. Examples include long-term loans and bond issues.
- Owner's equity represents the investment made by the owners plus profits that have been retained in the firm. Specifically, owner's equity includes the par value of all common stock issued, additional paid-in capital, and retained earnings.

4. Ratio Analysis

An evaluation of the relationships between financial statement variables is called a **ratio analysis**. The purpose of a financial ratio analysis is to identify the strengths and weaknesses of the firm.

4.1 Measures of Liquidity — indicate a firm's ability to meet short-term obligations
- Current ratio — reflects the relationship between current assets and current liabilities. A higher number means greater ability to cover short-term obligations.
- Quick ratio — similar to the current ratio, except that inventory is excluded in the calculation of current assets

4.2 Measures of Efficiency — indicate how well management is employing the firm's assets to generate revenue
- Inventory Turnover — measured as ratio of cost of goods sold to inventory; a higher number means that operations are supported with a lower inventory level (higher efficiency)
- Asset Turnover — measured as ratio of net sales to total assets; a higher number reflects more sales supported with a given level of assets (higher efficiency)

4.3 Measures of Financial Leverage — indicate degree to which assets are financed with debt
- Debt-to-equity ratio — high ratio reflects greater reliance on debt
- Times interest earned ratio — ability of the firm to cover its interest payments. A higher number means a higher level of income relative to interest payments and therefore greater ease of covering the debt payments.

4.4 Measures of Profitability — indicate management's ability to generate profits for owners of the firm
- Net profit margin — measures net income as a percentage of sales

- Return on assets (ROA) — measures net income as a percentage of the total assets utilized by the firm
- Return on equity (ROE) — measures net income as a percentage of the owner's investment in the business

4.5 Comparison of Ratios with Those of Other Firms
- Compare the ratios with other firms in the same industry or with an industry average.
- Compare ratios to those ratios in the past to determine how they have changed for the firm.

4.6 Limitations of Ratio Analysis
- Comparing a firm with an industry average is subject to error because many firms operate in more than one industry.
- Accounting practices vary among firms, which may cause a firm's ratios to deviate from the norm.
- Firms with seasonal variations in sales may show large deviations from the industry norm at certain times but not at others.

4.7 Sources of Information for Ratio Analysis
- The booklet *Annual Statement Studies*, published by **Robert Morris Associates**, provides financial ratios for many different industries.
- **Dun and Bradstreet** also provides financial ratios for selected industries, classified by size.

Solutions to End-of-Chapter Exercises

Concept Review Questions

(1) Business Valuation. What is accounting? Explain how managerial accounting can enhance the value of a firm.

Accounting is the summary and analysis of a firm's financial condition. Firms use accounting to report their financial condition, support decisions, and control the business. Effective managerial accounting can help a firm detect and correct deficiencies and therefore improve performance and enhance the firm's value.

(2) Auditing. Explain the role of auditing and why it is necessary.

Auditing refers to the assessment of the records that were used to prepare the firm's financial statements. Internal auditors specialize in evaluating the various divisions of a business to ensure that they are operating efficiently. Publicly traded firms must have their financial statements audited each year. The audit verifies that the financial statements are accurate.

(3) Sarbanes-Oxley Act. Describe the key provisions of the Sarbanes-Oxley Act that attempt to ensure the accuracy of financial statements created by publicly traded firms.

The key provisions of the act are:
- An auditing firm is allowed to provide nonaudit services when auditing a client only if the client's audit committee pre-approves the services.
- Auditing firms may not audit companies whose CEO, CFO, or other managers in similar roles were employed by the auditing firm in the year prior to the audit.
- The board members of a firm who are assigned to oversee the audit should not receive consulting or advising fees from the auditing firm.
- The CFO and other managers of the firm must file an internal control report along with each annual report.
- The CEO and CFO must certify that the audited statements fairly represent the operations and financial condition of the firm.

Major fines or prison terms are imposed on employees who mislead investors or hide evidence.

(4) Financial Statements. What is the difference between a balance sheet and an income statement?

The income statement indicates the revenue, expenses, and earnings (profits or net income) of a firm over a period of time (such as a quarter or year). The balance sheet reports the book value of all assets, liabilities, and owner's equity of a firm at a given point in time. It can be used to assess whether the firm has adequate liquidity and whether the firm has excessive debt.

(5) Income Statement. Show how an income statement can be broken down to determine a firm's gross profit. Once a firm has determined its gross profit, how would it compute its earnings before interest and taxes?

Net sales – cost of goods sold = gross profit.
Gross profit – operating expenses = earnings before interest and taxes.

(6) Motive for Assessing the Income Statement. What is the benefit of assessing an income statement?

An income statement can be used to assess a firm's sales, expenses, and earnings. It can indicate why its earnings are high or low.

(7) Financial Leverage. What do measures of financial leverage indicate? Why are they useful?

Financial leverage represents the degree to which a firm uses borrowed funds to finance its assets. Firms that borrow a large proportion of their funds have a high degree of financial leverage. Measuring financial leverage is important because it can indicate if a firm has a very high degree of debt, which could imply that the firm might have trouble meeting its debt payments in the future.

(8) Profitability. How can a firm's profitability be measured?

Profitability indicates the performance of a firm's operations during a given period of time. It can be measured with financial ratios such as the net profit margin, return on assets, or return on equity.

(9) Efficiency. Explain how a firm can use its reported sales and its assets to measure its efficiency.

A firm can measure its asset turnover, which is the ratio of net sales to total assets; a higher number reflects more sales supported with a given level of assets (higher efficiency).

(10) Ratio Analysis. What are the limitations of ratio analysis?

There are three key limitations of ratio analysis:
- Comparing a firm with an industry average is subject to error because many firms operate in more than one industry.
- Accounting practices vary among firms, which may cause a firm's ratios to deviate from the norm.
- Firms with seasonal variations in sales may show large deviations from the industry norm at certain times but not at others.

Class Communication Questions

(1) Sarbanes-Oxley Act. Some firms suggest that there is too much government regulation. The Sarbanes-Oxley Act has many rules that have increased the cost of reporting by more than $1 million per publicly traded firm on average. Do you think that these provisions are necessary?

Some students may suggest that the regulation is a waste. However, the intention of the act is to ensure proper financial reporting so that investors are not misled by false financial statements.

(2) Board Member Monitoring. The board members of a firm are sometimes given shares of the firm's stock as compensation. Board members are supposed to monitor the firm to ensure that managers serve the interests of shareholders. Do you think that board members can be trusted to monitor the firm's reporting process to ensure proper financial reporting?

When board members are paid with stock, they could benefit if financial reporting shows inflated earnings, because that may cause a high stock price (at least temporarily while investors are misled about the earnings) and allow them to sell their stock at a higher price.

(This occurred in the case of Enron.) Thus, some board members may not necessarily ensure that financial reporting is accurate.

(3) Balance Sheet Information. Why do you think creditors rely so heavily on a firm's balance sheet information when determining whether to provide the firm with a loan? Shouldn't the income statement be sufficient, since it indicates the firm's profitability?

An income statement does not indicate the firm's degree of financial leverage. A profitable firm may not be able to repay its debt in the future if it has substantial debt payments.

Small Business Case — Use of Financial Reporting for Business Decisions

Eight years ago, Sue and Jim Williams established the Surf Clothing Company, which produces clothing and then sells the clothing through their retail stores. Sue and Jim use an accounting system to keep track of revenue and expenses. First, the revenue and expenses are summed across all stores to provide an overall report. Second, revenue and expenses are reported per retail store so that an individual store's performance can be monitored. Third, revenue and expenses are reported per category of clothing (categorized by age group and gender) so that the performance of each clothing category can be monitored. This helps to identify the underlying reasons for the overall performance of the business.

(1) Use of Accounting to Assess Consumer Demand. How can the accounting system be used to compare consumer demand across the stores?

Revenue is based on demand by the local customers who shop at a particular store. The demand may be higher for stores when the income of local consumers is high, when the competition is low, and when the local customers have preferences for the type of clothing produced by the local store. By keeping track of revenue per store, the firm can determine where the demand is highest and lowest.

(2) How Financial Reporting Can Help Assess Managers. How can the accounting system be used to determine which stores deserve extra funding to support expansion?

The comparison of profits across stores can help determine which stores are performing relatively well and deserve to be expanded.

(3) How Financial Reporting Can Help Plan for Expansion. Sue and Jim Williams are planning to establish new clothing stores. First, they want to assess the performance of two stores that they opened earlier this year to detect any deficiencies in those stores that could be avoided in the new stores. How can accounting information be used to detect such deficiencies?

Accounting information can determine the main sources of a store's revenue, which may be used to determine the type of clothes that should be given the most room in new stores. However, the situation in one store may not indicate what will sell in other stores.

(4) How Ratio Analysis Can Guide Production Decisions. Explain how ratio analysis may affect the decision regarding the amount of clothing to order for the stores each month.

> Ratio analysis can determine each store's inventory level, which can indicate whether a store should replenish its inventory or still has sufficient inventory and can reduce its orders.

Web Insight — Financial Analysis at The Cheesecake Factory

At the opening of the chapter, The Cheesecake Factory was introduced. Use a search engine with the search terms "Cheesecake Factory" and "Investor Relations." This search will take you to the website where annual reports and other financial information are disclosed about The Cheesecake Factory. Summarize the type of financial information that is provided. Do you think most of this information reflects financial accounting (for the purpose of reporting to existing or prospective investors) or managerial accounting (for the purpose of helping the firm's managers make decisions)?

> The information provided reflects financial accounting because it is intended for existing or potential investors.

Dell's Secret for Success

Obtain a recent annual report of Dell and review the financial statements.

(1) Income Statement. What items on the income statement would Dell closely monitor to ensure that it was achieving its goals?

> Dell relies on efficient production so that it can still make profits even though its prices are low. So it would closely monitor its expenses. It would also assess its sales (revenue) over time.

(2) Balance Sheet. What balance sheet items would be very important to Dell?

> Dell would pay close attention to the amount of cash that it has, its long-term assets, and its debt.

(3) Financial Reporting. Review Dell's comments about its financial reporting. Why is it important for Dell to inform investors about its efforts to monitor and control its financial reporting?

> Dell recognizes that mistakes can happen in the process of financial reporting. Dell wants to convince investors that its financial statements are accurate.

Video Exercise — Lessons in Financial Analysis

Many free business videos are available on websites such as YouTube (www.youtube.com), and more are added every day. Search for a recent video clip about an existing business that offers lessons on "company financial analysis" or "company financial accounting" in YouTube or any other website that provides video clips.

(1) Main Lesson. What is the name of the business in the video clip? Is the video clip focused on why the firm conducts a financial analysis of its business, or how it conducts an analysis, or some other aspect of financial analysis? What is the main lesson of the video clip that you watched?

Answers will vary among students. The main point is to ensure that students take the initiative to access and watch a related video and recognize the main lesson provided by the video.

(2) Recording Financial Information. Some small companies maintain only enough financial information to determine what taxes they owe on their income. Explain how financial information could be used by even small (private) businesses to improve their performance.

Financial information can determine whether a firm holds enough cash and inventory to avoid shortages. It can also determine whether the firm is using its assets efficiently and whether it should have adequate future income to cover its debt payments.

(3) Use of Financial Information for Planning. How can a firm use financial information to assess the accuracy of its business plan?

Within a firm's business plan, there are financial projections. A firm can compare its actual financial situation to its projections to determine whether its projections were accurate. This is relevant because it can help a firm derive more accurate financial projections as it revises its business plan for the future.

Chapter 16: Financing

Introduction

The **Learning Objectives** for this chapter are to:

1. Identify the common methods of debt financing for firms.

2. Identify the common methods of equity financing for firms.

3. Explain how firms issue securities to obtain funds.

4. Explain how firms may obtain financing through suppliers or leasing.

5. Describe how firms determine the composition of their financing.

6. Describe the remedies for firms that are unable to repay their debts.

1. Methods of Debt Financing
Debt financing is the act of borrowing funds.

1.1 Borrowing from Financial Institutions
- Collateral — commonly the asset purchased with the borrowed funds. This reduces the risk of default for the lender
- Loan rate — may be based on the **prime rate** (rate charged on loans to the most creditworthy firms). The higher the credit risk of the firm, the larger the risk premium added to the prime rate
- Fixed-rate loan versus floating-rate loan — the choice is largely determined by anticipated future interest rate movements, which are always subject to uncertainty

1.2. Issuing Bonds — long-term debt instruments (IOUs) sold to investors
- Par value of a bond — amount that bondholders receive at maturity
- Coupon payments — payments provided semiannually to bondholders
- Indenture — legal contract that describes the firm's obligations to bondholders, including:
  - Whether the bond is secured (backed by collateral) or unsecured (backed only by the general creditworthiness of the firm)
  - Whether the bond has a call feature that provides the issuing firm with the right to repurchase the bonds before maturity
  - Protective covenants that impose restrictions on specific financial policies of the firm (may restrict the firm from acquiring additional debt until the existing bonds are paid off)

147

1.3 Issuing Commercial Paper — short-term debt security issued by firms in good financial condition

1.4 Impact of the Debt Financing Level on Interest Expenses

1.5 Common Creditors That Provide Debt Financing:
- Commercial banks — provide business loans
- Savings institutions — accept deposits from individuals and provide business loans
- They also provide home mortgages for individuals
- Finance companies — lend most of their funds to businesses
- Pension funds — purchase bonds issued by firms
- Insurance companies — purchase bonds issued by firms
- Bond mutual funds — purchase bonds issued by firms

2. **Methods of Equity Financing**

2.1 Retained Earnings — many firms retain a portion of their earnings to invest in existing operations or expansion of business

2.2 Issuing Stock
Common stock represents partial ownership in the issuing corporation. Preferred stock offers specific priorities over common stock.
- Issuing stock to venture capital firms allows a firm to sell stock to a selected group of investors. Venture capital firms consist of individuals who invest in small, potentially profitable businesses.
- An initial public offering (IPO) is the first issue of common stock, also called "going public." An IPO allows a firm to obtain funding without increasing its debt level.

Disadvantages of IPOs:
- Firm must disclose financial information to the public.
- Firm may have difficulty attracting funds from investors.
- Dilution of ownership as new stock is sold to new investors.
- Investment banks charge high fees for placing new stock with investors.

Listing of the stock — most popular stock exchanges in the United States are the New York Stock Exchange (NYSE), NYSE Alternext U.S. (formed after NYSE Euronext acquired the American Stock Exchange, AMEX), and the over-the-counter (OTC) market.

2.3 Comparison of Equity Financing with Debt Financing.

3. **How Firms Issue Securities**
A public offering is the selling of securities to the general public

3.1 Origination — advising by investment banks on the amount of securities to issue and the offer price.

3.2 Underwriting
When security offerings are **underwritten**, the investment bank guarantees a price to the issuing firm, no matter what price the securities may sell for. Alternatively, the investment bank may sell the issue on a **best-efforts basis**. In this case, the investment banker does not guarantee a price to the issuing firm.

3.3 Distribution
The issuing firm must provide the Securities and Exchange Commission (SEC) with a **prospectus** (document that discloses relevant financial information regarding the securities and the issuing corporation). In the distribution of securities, **flotation costs** are fees paid by the issuing firm to investment banks for advice, marketing, printing expenses, and registration fees.

Some firms prefer to use a **private placement**, in which the securities are sold to one or a few investors.

4. Other Methods of Obtaining Funds

4.1 Financing from Suppliers

4.2 Leasing — can provide a firm with the use of an asset without the large initial outlay of funds necessary to purchase the asset

5. Deciding the Capital Structure
A firm's capital structure is the amount of debt versus equity financing. Debt provides the firm with tax-deductible interest payments. But excessive debt can increase the risk of default. Equity funding provides no tax deduction, but the firm is not required to repay the investment by owners

5.1 Revising the Capital Structure — if interest rates decline, firms may increase the amount of debt in their capital structure

5.2 How the Capital Structure Affects the Return on Equity — Higher debt can achieve a higher return on equity. However, higher debt also increases the risk of default on debt payments.

6. Remedies for Debt Problems

6.1 Extension — provides additional time to obtain cash that is needed

6.2 Composition — the firm agrees to pay part of what it owes

6.3 Private Liquidation — the firm and its creditors informally agree on how to liquidate its assets and allocate the proceeds among the creditors

6.4 Formal Remedies
- Reorganization — restructuring plan must be agreed to by firm and creditors
- Liquidation under bankruptcy — a law firm will be hired to liquidate assets and allocate funds to creditors

Appendix: How Interest Rates Are Determined

A.1 How Interest Rates Change
- Interest rates are influenced by supply of loanable funds and demand for those funds.
- Interest rates are determined by the interaction of the demand and supply schedules for loanable funds. The interest rate at which the quantity of loanable funds supplied is equal to the quantity of loanable funds demanded is the **equilibrium interest rate**.
- When the demand schedule of loanable funds changes, there is a change in the equilibrium interest rate.

A.2 Factors That Can Affect Interest Rates
- The Federal Reserve System can increase the supply of loanable funds, which will reduce the equilibrium interest rate.
- An increase in economic growth can increase the demand for loanable funds, which will increase the equilibrium interest rate.
- When consumers expect an increase in inflation, they tend to borrow more money, and this increases the demand for loanable funds and the equilibrium interest rate.
- When people save more money, the supply of loanable funds increases, and this will reduce the equilibrium interest rate.

Solutions to End-of-Chapter Exercises

Concept Review Questions

(1) Collateral. Explain the role of collateral and how it can make it easier for a business to obtain a loan.

Collateral represents assets used by a firm to back a loan it receives. Thus, if a business uses the loan to purchase an office building, it may use the building as collateral. If the firm defaults on payments, the lender will take ownership of the building. Some lenders require collateral before they will provide a loan. In addition, the lender may offer a lower interest rate when the loan is backed with collateral, because it has less to lose.

(2) Prime Rate. What is the prime rate, and how is it used to set rates on loans to businesses?

The prime rate is the interest rate charged on loans to the most creditworthy firms. The higher the credit risk of a firm, the higher the premium above the prime rate that will be charged by a lender for a loan.

(3) Floating-Rate Loan. Explain how a firm's interest expenses would change during a four-year period of rising interest rates if it obtains a floating-rate loan at the beginning of the period.

If interest rates rise, the interest rate on a floating-rate loan will be periodically adjusted upward. Thus, the interest expense on a floating-rate loan will rise over time.

(4) Bonds. Explain why firms issue bonds. What is par value? What are protective covenants?

A firm issues bonds to obtain debt financing. The firm will need to pay coupon payments each year. The par value of a bond is the amount that bondholders receive at maturity. Protective covenants impose restrictions on specific financial policies of the firm (may restrict a firm from acquiring additional debt until the existing bonds are paid off).

(5) Secured Versus Unsecured Bonds. Explain the difference between secured and unsecured bonds.

Secured bonds are backed by collateral. Unsecured bonds are backed only by the general creditworthiness of the firm. A call feature provides the issuing firm with the right to repurchase the bonds before maturity.

(6) Indenture. When a firm plans to issue bonds, what is the role of an indenture?

When a firm plans to issue bonds, it creates an indenture, which is a legal contract that describes the firm's obligations to bondholders. It identifies the collateral used to secure the bonds. It states whether the bonds can be called, and may specify restrictions on the firm regarding specific financial policies. These restrictions, called protective covenants, are intended to protect the interests of the bondholders.

(7) Financial Institutions. Identify the common types of financial institutions that serve as creditors for firms.

The common types of financial institutions that provide loans directly to firms are commercial banks, savings institutions, and finance companies. In addition, pension funds, insurance companies, and bond mutual funds commonly serve as creditors by purchasing bonds issued by firms.

(8) Equity Financing. What are the two common methods that firms use to obtain equity financing?

A firm can retain earnings, which are profits that the firm reinvests rather than distributing them to shareholders. In addition, the firm can issue stock.

(9) Initial Public Offering. What is an initial public offering (IPO)? What are some disadvantages of engaging in an IPO?

An initial public offering (IPO) is the first issue of common stock. Disadvantages of IPOs are as follows:
- Firm must disclose financial information to the public.
- Firm may have difficulty attracting funds from investors.
- Dilution of ownership as new stock is sold to new investors.
- Investment banks charge high fees for placing new stock with investors.

(10) Debt Financing. Why would owners of a firm prefer to use debt financing rather than equity financing?

The original owners of the firm may want to retain all ownership. In addition, the debt payments are tax deductible.

Class Communication Questions

(1) Going Public. You are one of 10 owners of a business that has expanded substantially and has performed very well. You and the other owners have complete control of the business and are very focused on making the business efficient. Some of the owners want to go public so that they can sell their ownership shares to other investors. There are many small investors who do not know the business very well but who would invest in shares in the hope of earning a high return on their investment. Do you think going public will improve the performance of the business?

If some owners sell their ownership, they will no longer have an interest in running the business. This could adversely affect the business. In addition, the new owners may want to have some input on how the business should be managed, and they may not have any insight on how the business should be run.

(2) Dividends. You are a financial manager of a publicly traded firm. You expect that the firm will expand its business substantially in the future but it already has a lot of debt. Do you think the firm should distribute most of its future earnings as dividends? Explain.

The firm will need funding for its expansion, so it should retain most or all of its earnings in order to support the expansion.

(3) Funding Dilemma. Your friend wants to expand his small business. There is considerable risk that the business might fail if economic conditions weaken. Yet, your friend has very little of his own money invested in the business. A financial institution is willing to provide him with a loan, but at a very high interest rate. He thinks that he should accept the loan. He says that if the business fails, the lender will be the loser because he does not have much money invested in the business. Will you advise your friend to accept the loan?

Small Business Case — Financing Decisions

Rock-On Company produces musical instruments, including guitars and drum sets, and sells them to retail stores in North Carolina. It currently has 30 owners who have already invested a total of $4 million in the firm. It used the equity to invest in its operations. Now Rock-On wants to purchase an additional manufacturing plant that will cost about $4 million. It has about $1 million in cash retained from recent earnings, so it will need to borrow the remaining $3 million to purchase this plant. If Rock-On obtains a loan, it will have to make loan payments of about $300,000 a year.

(1) Use of a Business Plan to Obtain a Loan. If Rock-On Company pursues a loan, why would a lender require it to provide a financial plan showing how the funds would be used?

The lender wants to determine whether the planned use of the funds will likely generate sufficient funds that will allow the firm to repay the loan.

(2) Impact of Firm's Condition on Its Loan Rate. Why would the interest rate charged on a loan to Rock-On Company be dependent on its financial condition?

Lenders charge a loan rate that reflects the risk of default on a loan. If a borrower is more risky, it will have to pay a higher premium (above the prevailing risk-free interest rate) that reflects the potential for default.

(3) Equity Financing Tradeoff. Instead of borrowing to obtain funds to purchase an additional manufacturing plant, Rock-On Company is considering using equity funding to finance this investment. It could obtain additional equity from a venture capital firm. What is the potential advantage of obtaining equity rather than borrowing funds? What is the disadvantage of using equity financing?

If the firm obtains equity, it will not need to borrow funds, so it will not need to make interest payments. However, it will reduce the proportional ownership of existing investors.

(4) Leasing Decision. If Rock-On Company wants the flexibility to expand a specific production facility it is using, would it prefer to purchase (own) or lease the facility?

It would prefer to purchase the facility so that it can revise the facility as it wishes.

Web Insight — eBay's IPO

At the opening of the chapter, eBay was introduced. Recall that eBay engaged in an initial public offering (IPO) in September 1998. Investors who were able to purchase eBay's stock at the time of the IPO earned a very high return on their investment in eBay in a single day.
Conduct an online search using the search terms "eBay" and "IPO" and review information about eBay's IPO. By how much did eBay's price rise on the day of the IPO?

When eBay engaged in an IPO, the initial offer price was $18 per share. The stock's price by the end of the day was $47.37 per share. The price increased by 163% in one day, which means that for an investor who invested $10,000 in the stock at the time of the IPO, the stock was worth $26,317 by the end of the day.

Dell's Secret for Success

Go to Dell's website (www.dell.com) and click on the link "About Dell," near the bottom of the web page. You can also review an annual report to obtain more information.

(1) Capital Structure. Some firms rely more on debt than on equity as a source of funds. Dell tends to use a relatively small amount of debt compared to its equity. What is the advantage of this strategy?

Dell relies on just a small amount of debt relative to its equity, so it has more flexibility to borrow in the future if it needs more funds.

(2) Initial Public Offering. Dell's website describes its initial public offering in 1988, just four years after its business was created. It raised $30 million from its offering. Why do you think Dell needed to issue stock?

Dell was expanding at the time and would not have been able to borrow such a large amount of funds.

Video Exercise — Lessons in Business Financing

Many free business videos are available on websites such as YouTube (www.youtube.com), and more are added every day. Search for a recent video clip about an existing business that offers lessons on "business financing" in YouTube or any other website that provides video clips.

(1) Main Lesson. What is the name of the business in the video clip? Is the video clip focused on why financing is critical to the business, or how much financing it needs, or how it determines the composition of its financing, or some other aspect of business financing? What is the main lesson of the video clip that you watched?

Answers will vary among students. The main point is to ensure that students take the initiative to access and watch a related video and recognize the main lesson provided by the video.

(2) Debt Financing. Some related videos illustrate how a business can experience problems if it obtains only debt financing and no equity financing. Explain why a business could experience financial problems when most of its financing is with debt.

If a business relies heavily on debt financing, it must make large interest payments to creditors. In some periods when the demand for the firm's products is low (perhaps due to a slow economy), its revenue will decline, but it must still make its interest payments on debt. Thus, it may not have sufficient cash from revenue to make its interest payments and cover all of its other expenses. If it does not have high interest payments, it may more easily be able to cover all of its expenses.

(3) Excessive Financing. Some related videos explain how firms that recently experienced strong growth engage in stock offerings to support future growth. Is it possible for a business to obtain more funds than it needs? If so, how could this adversely affect the business?

If a business obtains funding from a stock offering, but its growth slows, it may not need to expand its operations as initially planned. If it uses the funds to expand anyway, this will be a waste of funds, because the firm will have more facilities and machinery than it needs. If it does not use the funds to expand, but just places them in a bank account, it will be earning a very small return on these funds. The investors who provided these funds would not have invested the money if they knew the firm was just going to place the funds in a bank account.

Chapter 17: Expanding the Business

Introduction

The **Learning Objectives** for this chapter are to:

1. Explain capital budgeting and identify the types of investment decisions that a firm may make.

2. Describe the capital budgeting tasks that are necessary to make business investment decisions.

3. Describe the motive for investing in other firms, explain the merger process, and identify other types of restructuring that firms may use..

4. Explain how firms make decisions for investing in short-term assets.

1. Investment Decisions

Capital budgeting involves a comparison of the costs and benefits of proposed investment projects to determine whether the investment is feasible
- Costs — initial outlay as well as any costs incurred over the life of the project
- Benefits — cash flows generated by the project

1.1 How Interest Rates Affect Investment Decisions
Firms must earn a return on investment from projects that exceeds their cost of funds invested. The cost of funds is influenced by the cost of borrowing.

1.2 Capital Budget — a firm's targeted amount of funds to be used for purchasing assets such as buildings, machinery, and equipment that are needed for long-term projects

1.3 Classification of Capital Expenditures
- Expansion of current business
- Development of new business
- Investment in assets that will enable the firm to reduce expenses

2. Capital Budgeting Tasks
The capital budgeting process involves five tasks

2.1 Proposing New Projects

2.2 Estimating Cash Flows of Each Project.

2.3 Determining Whether Proposals Are Feasible
- Mutually exclusive projects — projects that are designed to achieve the same objective
- Independent projects — projects that are unrelated, so adopting one project is independent of the decision about the other project

2.4 Implementing Feasible Projects

2.5 Monitoring Projects That Were Implemented

2.6 Summary of Capital Budgeting Tasks

3. **Mergers**

   3.1 Types of Mergers:
   - horizontal merger — combination of firms engaged in the same type of business
   - vertical merger — combination of firms in which one firm is a potential supplier or customer of the other firm
   - conglomerate merger — combination between firms in unrelated businesses. The merger of a snack food manufacturer with a producer of automotive parts would be a conglomerate merger

   3.2 Corporate Motives for Mergers
   - Immediate growth
   - Economies of scale — reduce costs and operate more efficiently by eliminating duplicate resources
   - Managerial expertise — poorly managed companies have low value and are attractive takeover targets for firms that could replace management and improve value. Some mergers capitalize on the managerial expertise of the target
   - Tax benefits — targets with losses can reduce the taxes of the acquiring firm

   3.3 Merger Analysis
   - Identify merger prospects
   - Evaluate potential merger prospects
   - Make the merger decision

   3.4 Merger Procedures
   - Financing the merger — a firm can issue shares of its own stock and use the proceeds to buy the stock of the target firm. It can also use cash. In some cases, it uses mostly

borrowed funds. A leveraged buyout (LBO) is a purchase of a company (or the subsidiary of a company) by a group of investors using borrowed funds.

- Bidding process — if both parties do not agree to the merger, the acquiring firm can make a bid for shares of stock in the target firm and attemps to obtain control in this manner
- Integrating the business — a key to this process is to clearly communicate the strategic plan. There are likely to be some tensions and difficulties while the reorganization is completed.
- Postmerger evaluation — the firm should periodically assess the merger's costs and benefits after the merger in order to learn from the process in case it pursues another merger in the future

3.5 Target's Defense Against Takeover Attempts
- Target may convince existing stockholders to retain their shares.
- Target may engage in a private placement of stock. It sells shares of stock to selected institutions that will not sell their stock. This prevents the acquiring firm from purchasing enough shares of stock to gain a controlling interest.
- Target may find a more suitable company (called a **white knight**) to acquire it.

4. Short-Term Investment Decisions
Working capital management is the management of a firm's short-term assets and liabilities.

4.1 Liquidity Management
Firms manage their short-term assets and liabilities to ensure adequate liquidity.

Firms invest in Treasury bills (short-term debt securities offered by the U.S. Treasury) because they are safe and can easily be sold to other investors. However, Treasury bills and other short-term assets typically offer low returns, so firms attempt to hold just enough to ensure adequate liquidity.

Firms typically arrange for a line of credit with one or more banks in order to access funds when needed.

4.2 Accounts Receivable Management
Firms set limits on the amount of credit available to customers and the length of time before payment is due. Allowing credit may generate more sales, but it results in delayed payments and possibly defaults on payments. Firms should ensure that customers are creditworthy.

4.3 Inventory Management
A large inventory avoids the risk of stockouts, but it ties up more funds that could have been invested in other projects.

Solutions to End-of-Chapter Exercises

Concept Review Questions

(1) Feasibility of a Project. Explain how a capital budgeting decision determines whether a proposed business project is feasible. Why might the prevailing interest rate influence a firm's decision to invest in a new project?

Capital budgeting involves a comparison of the costs and benefits of a proposed investment in order to determine if a proposed project is feasible. Costs include the initial outlay as well as any costs incurred over the life of the project. Benefits include cash flows generated by the project. A firm should only pursue projects in which the benefits exceed the costs. The prevailing interest rate can affect the required rate of return of the business because it affects the cost of financing the project. A high required rate of return could cause a business to reject some projects that might have been feasible if the required return was lower.

(2) Capital Expenditures. Describe the common types of capital expenditures by a business.

The common types of expenditures include:
- Expansion of current business to grow the business.
- Development of new business to expand into new types of products.
- Investment in assets that will enable the firm to reduce expenses.

(3) Capital Budgeting Tasks. Describe the tasks involved in capital budgeting.

The capital budgeting process involves five tasks:
- Propose new projects.
- Estimate cash flows of each project.
- Determine which proposals are feasible.
- Implement feasible projects.
- Monitor the projects that were implemented.

(4) Mutually Exclusive Projects. Explain the difference between mutually exclusive projects and independent projects that are considered by businesses.

Mutually exclusive projects are designed to achieve the same objective, so the selection of one of these projects would preclude the need for the others.

Independent projects are not designed to achieve the same objective. Adopting one project is independent of the decision about the other project.

(5) Types of Mergers. Describe the common types of mergers.

The common types of mergers are:
- **Horizontal merger** — combination of firms engaged in the same type of business
- **Vertical merger** — combination of firms in which one firm is a potential supplier or customer of the other firm
- **Conglomerate merger** — between firms in unrelated businesses. The merger of a snack food manufacturer with a producer of automotive parts would be a conglomerate merger.

(6) Motives for Mergers. What are common motives for corporate mergers?

Motives for mergers include:
- Immediate growth
- Economies of scale — reduce costs and operate more efficiently by eliminating duplicate resources
- Managerial expertise — poorly managed companies have low value and are attractive takeover targets for firms that could replace management and improve value. Some mergers capitalize on the managerial expertise of the target.
- Tax benefits — targets with losses can reduce the taxes of the acquiring firm

(7) Methods to Finance a Merger. Explain common methods used to finance a merger.

A firm can issue shares of its own stock and use the proceeds to buy the stock of the target firm. It can also use cash.

In some cases, a firm uses mostly borrowed funds. A **leveraged buyout (LBO)** is a purchase of a company (or the subsidiary of a company) by a group of investors using borrowed funds.

(8) Divestiture Motives. Why might a firm divest some of its assets?

A firm may divest a business when:
- It decides that the assets to be divested do not fit with the rest of its operations,
- It needs cash and the sale of the assets can provide it with the cash it needs,
- It believes the assets are worth more if sold than retained.

(9) Liquidity Management. Describe a firm's liquidity management.

Liquidity management involves the management of the firm's short-term assets and liabilities to ensure adequate liquidity. Firms invest in **Treasury bills** (short-term debt securities offered by the U.S. Treasury) because they are safe and can easily be sold to other investors. However, Treasury bills and other short-term assets typically offer low returns, so firms attempt to hold just enough to ensure adequate liquidity. Firms typically arrange for a **line of credit** with one or more banks in order to access funds when needed.

(10) Credit Policy. Describe a firm's accounts receivable management and explain the tradeoff involved when a firm allows no credit versus when it uses a liberal credit policy.

A firm's accounts receivable management sets limits on the amount of credit available to customers and the length of time before payment is due. Allowing credit may generate more sales, but it results in delayed payments and possibly defaults on payments. Firms may ensure that customers are creditworthy.

Class Communication Questions

(1) Merger Strategy. A firm notices that one of its competitors has performed well. It decides to acquire this other firm to improve its own performance. Why might this effort backfire?

The target firm can command a high price because it has performed well recently. So the expense of acquiring the target could exceed the potential benefits.

(2) Credit Policy. To increase sales, a firm decides to extend credit to all customers and not to require payment until one year after the products are purchased. Does this liberal credit policy make sense? Justify your opinion.

This policy could backfire. Customers may never make their payments. The firm should only consider a credit policy for creditworthy customers.

(3) Inventory Policy. A retail firm wants to ensure that it will not run out of inventory of televisions. It usually sells about 100 televisions per week. The firm decides to build a huge warehouse that can store 3,000 televisions so that it will not experience stockouts. Does this inventory policy make sense? Justify your opinion.

The inventory policy is inefficient because it will tie up funds invested in the huge warehouse and in the televisions and those funds could have been used in better ways.

Small Business Case — Deciding Whether to Acquire a Business

Benson, Inc., is a publisher of books that it sells to retail bookstores in the United States. Judith Benson, the owner, is concerned because her suppliers continue to increase the price of paper and other materials that her company purchases from them weekly. One supplier to Benson, Inc., is Hill Company, which provides high-quality supplies but has experienced financial problems recently because of inefficient management.

Judith believes that Benson could benefit from merging with Hill Company. She believes that she could acquire (purchase) Hill Company at a low price because it has performed poorly in the past. She also believes that she could improve Hill's performance by reorganizing its business. In addition, the merger with Hill would give Benson, Inc., more control over the cost of its supplies. It could obtain supplies from Hill, which would now be part of Benson, Inc. Therefore, it would not be subject to increased prices by other suppliers. Meanwhile, Hill would not only produce supplies for Benson, but would also sell them to other customers, as it did in the past.

(1) Type of Merger. What type of merger is Judith considering?

This merger would be a vertical merger because it reflects a merger between a firm and its supplier.

(2) Pricing the Target. Explain the key factors that Judith should consider when deciding on the price to offer for the target (Hill Company).

Judith could estimate the cash flows would result from the merger. She should also consider the costs that she would incur as a result of the merger, including any cost of restructuring Hill Company.

(3) Risk of a Merger. How could the purchase of Hill Company backfire?

If the cash flows are not as high as expected, the benefits of this merger may be negative. That is, the extra cash flows resulting from the merger would not be sufficient to recapture the initial outlay required to buy Hill Company.

Web Insight — Business Expansion at Netflix

At the opening of the chapter, Netflix was introduced. Go to the website (http://ir.netflix.com/annuals.cfm) to retrieve a recent annual report (or you can find the information by using the search terms "Netflix" and "annual report" on a search engine). Review Nexflix's most recent letter to shareholders, which is at the beginning of its annual report. Summarize the comments made by Netflix about its recent growth and plans for future expansion.

Netflix has grown substantially and still has plans to grow. It especially has potential for growing in international markets.

Dell's Secret for Success

Go to Dell's website (www.dell.com) and click on the link "About Dell," near the bottom of the web page. You can also review a recent annual report to obtain more information.

(1) Type of Expansion. Dell has expanded its operations in recent years. Review how the size of Dell's assets has increased over time.

Dell has expanded across the country and into other countries, and it has expanded its product line.

163

(2) Reasons for Growth. Why do you think Dell has been able to grow at a much faster rate than other firms in its industry?

> Dell has kept its prices relatively low and has maintained high quality, so it continues to attract more customers over time. It has also expanded overseas and therefore tapped into new markets as a result of its expansion.

(3) Dell's Potential Growth. Do you think Dell is reaching its peak level, or does it have more potential for growth?

> Dell could expand more by adding more products to its product line or by expanding into some other countries that may develop in the future.

Video Exercise — Lessons in Business Acquisitions

Many free business videos are available on websites such as YouTube (www.youtube.com), and more are added every day. Search for a recent video clip about an existing business that offers lessons on "company's acquisition" in YouTube or any other website that provides video clips.

(1) Main Lesson. What is the name of the business in the video clip? Is the video clip focused on the potential benefits of merging with another business, or the process the firm used to engage in an acquisition, or some other aspect of business acquisitions? What is the main lesson of the video clip that you watched?

> Answers will vary among students. The main point is to ensure that students take the initiative to access and watch a related video and recognize the main lesson provided by the video.

(2) Why Acquisitions Can Backfire. Some acquisitions have backfired as the performance of the acquiring firm deteriorated after it acquired the target. Why do you think some acquisitions backfire?

> Many answers are possible but one of the most common problems is that the acquiring firm was overly optimistic about the potential benefits and paid too much money to purchase the target company. Another common problem is that merging the employees of two firms is difficult. For example, if departments of both firms are merged, employees may be concerned that they will be laid off. Therefore, they focus more on protecting their jobs and less on making the acquisition successful.

(3) Benefits of Communication. Some businesses tha havet merged emphasize the importance of communicating to all employees the plans following the acquisition. Why is communication so important?

> Employees may fear that they will be laid off after the acquisition when some departments are consolidated. The high-level managers should communicate whether there will be layoffs

so that employees will know what to expect. This may reduce the concerns of some employees, and allow them to focus on their work rather than on worrying about losing their jobs.

Solutions to End-of-Part Exercises (Part VI)

Video on Managing a Business — Financing for Success

The Small Business Administration (SBA) plays a very important role in helping many small businesses. Its website, which offers a wide range of services and information for small businesses, has a section called Delivering Success (www.sba.gov/tools/audiovideo/ deliveringsuccess/index.html) that provides video clips of small business success stories. Go to this website, and watch the video called "Entrepreneurial Spirit" (total time of clip is 5 minutes, 49 seconds).

In this video clip, an entrepreneur of a successful business summarizes his experience and offers advice about financing a small business. A small business needs to develop a well-organized plan to obtain a loan from a bank. The future revenue and some expenses of a business cannot be forecasted with perfect accuracy, so the small business owner must consider how the business's performance might change under alternative conditions (such as an increase in competition, a weakening of the economy, etc.). The entrepreneur obtained financing for his small business with the help of an SBA guarantee backing his business. That is, if his business defaulted on the loan, the SBA would pay off the loan. Thus, the commercial bank was more willing to offer financing for the small business.

(1) Interaction Between Accounting and Financing. Explain the relationship between the accounting function (Chapter 15) of a business and the financing function (Chapter 16). Why is the accounting function necessary for a business in order to obtain financing?

The accounting function is used to develop financial projections of costs and revenue, and the financial statements derived from this function can be part of the financial plan. A bank that provides financing will require a small business to disclose its projected costs and revenue and to justify its projections.

(2) How Short-term Investment Decisions Are Influenced by Access to Financing. Explain how the firm's short-term investment decisions (Chapter 17) are related to its access to financing (Chapter 17).

If a firm has easy access to bank financing, it can survive with less cash and marketable securities. Conversely, if the firm does not have easy access to bank financing, it needs to maintain more cash and marketable securities. If it suddenly needs funds, it can use the cash and can sell the marketable securities for cash.

(3) How Acquisition and Financing Decisions Are Related. Explain how acquisitions (Chapter 17) are dependent on financing (Chapter 16).

An acquisition commonly requires that one firm borrow funds that it uses to purchase the other firm. Thus, an acquisition may be mostly funded with borrowed funds. Banks and other creditors will provide funding only if they believe that the firm borrowing the money will be capable of paying off the loan over time. Thus, the firm must demonstrate that it will be able to repay the loan.